KAFFE FASSETT'S QUILTS IN LONDON

Photographed at Camden Lock Market

featuring
Liza Prior Lucy
Brandon Mably

location photography
Debbie Patterson

An imprint of **ABRAMS**
abramsbooks.com

First published in the USA in 2025

Patchwork designs	Kaffe Fassett Liza Prior Lucy
Quilt making coordination	Heart Space Studios (UK) Liza Prior Lucy (US)
Technical editor	Bundle Backhouse
Designer Art direction/styling	Anne Wilson Kaffe Fassett
Location photography Additional photography	Debbie Patterson Brandon Mably (pp 7T; 8; 9BR) Dorothy Hill (pp 4; 152)
Stills photography	Steven Wooster
Quilt illustrations	Heart Space Studios
Publishing consultant	Susan Berry (Berry & Co)

ISBN: 978-1-4197-8469-9

Library of Congress Control Number In progress

Colour reproduction	Pixywalls Ltd, London

Printed in China
10 9 8 7 6 5 4 3 2 1

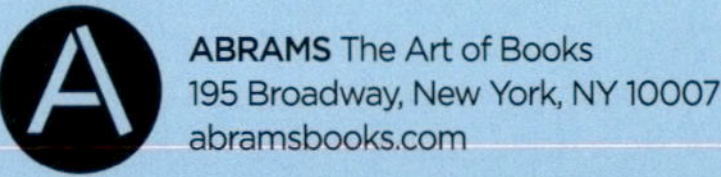

ABRAMS The Art of Books
195 Broadway, New York, NY 10007
abramsbooks.com

Page 1: The waters of the Regent's Canal make a great backdrop for my *Mossy Bordered Diamonds* quilt.
Right: The fussy-cut central squares in my *Hot Economy* quilt really zing out.

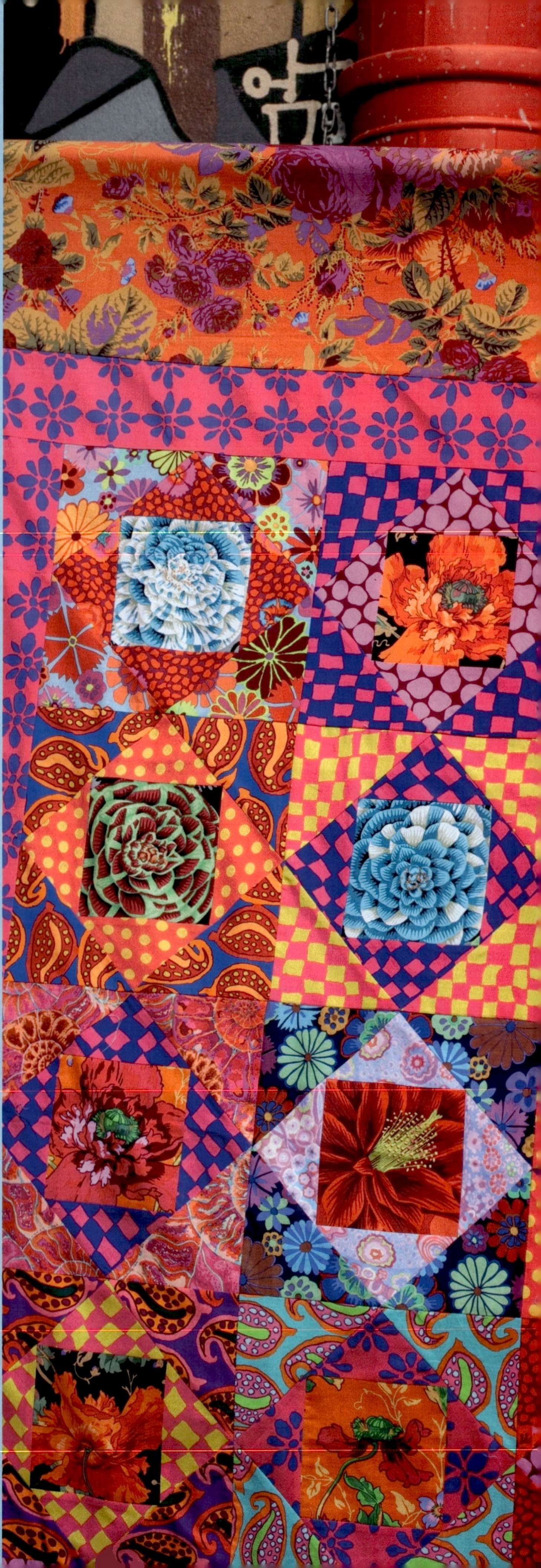

Contents

introduction

One of the benefits of reaching my great age is that I have lived through so many different waves of youthful expression. My first memories were of the 'Beat' generation, which saw the emergence of poets, singers and authors who exerted a huge influence on the culture of the time. Then came the hippies, who really shook up the status quo, particularly in America. In England, where I now live, we had the Beatles who brought a gentle fantasy to the party. The goths, romantics and punks followed, but I was less involved with those movements.

In London, Camden Lock Market on the Regent's Canal – a favourite backdrop for these successive groups – has become increasingly popular over recent years and now attracts new young trend seekers from every corner of the globe. I love seeing their show-stopping get-ups with coloured hair and fanciful clothing. The Market panders to this thirst for fun, providing exotic props in an ongoing display. Great crowds mill about, fascinated by the extreme apparel on offer while salivating over the waves of enticing aromas from the

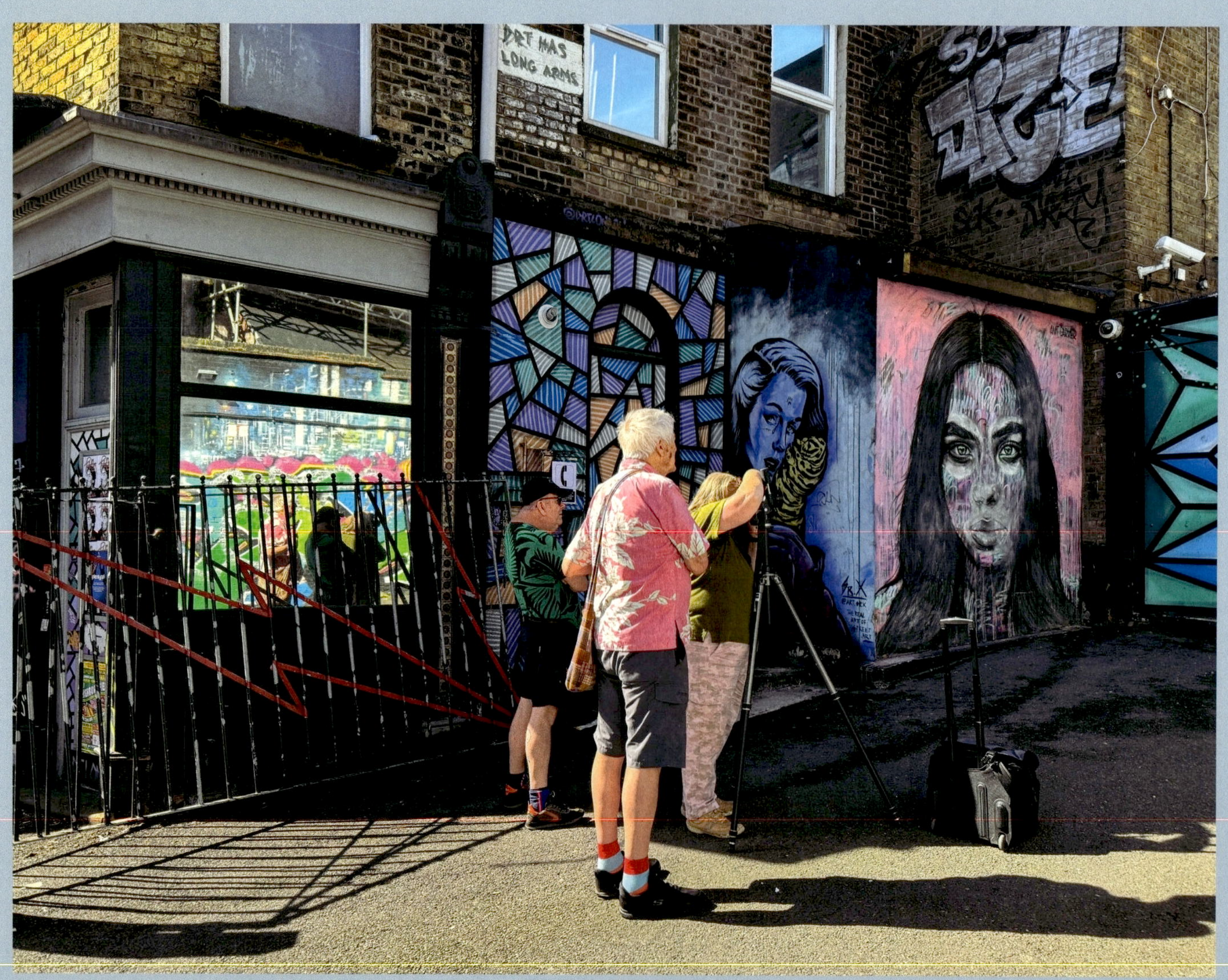

many food stalls doing bustling business. This heightened lifestyle invites everyone to join in the carnival-like atmosphere. With the shops outdoing themselves to attract the crowds, we end up with a street that begins to feel more like a circus or fun fair.

My partner, Brandon, and I spent hours exploring the area, and the Regent's Canal that runs through it, as a location for this year's quilt photography. One great bonus of Camden's celebration of creativity is the plethora of murals that artists worldwide have been encouraged to produce as a background to this now internationally renowned market. So, in place of most cities' depressingly grey concrete walls, here in Camden we get great colourful fantasies. This made it wonderfully exciting for us as we could show off our quilts on backgrounds that magnified the colours and patterns in each.

Within the small area of the booming market, we found most of our settings as if they had been made to order. Plus, when exploring the canal, we found a community of canal-boat dwellers whose boats and lifestyle provided another charming setting for some of our quilts.

Each season when our latest collection of prints is delivered to the studio, Brandon and I create quilts that we feel show them off to their best advantage. We've noticed that each colour grouping creates quite a distinct

mood, from cool to hot palettes, moving from delicate pastels to deep, rich shades. So, in this book I decided to emphasize those varying moods by limiting the number of blocks we used in the quilt designs, and by showing each block in three different colour moods. This demonstrates very clearly how basic layouts can be transformed by each change of colour mood.

Liza Lucy, my co-designer, chose to take a different route towards the same goal. She, too, took a single block theme – a snowball – but then rang the changes in the snowball block layout. She used a soft, more neutral palette for two of her designs but created an explosion of hot colours in the third.

We decided to finish and quilt only the main design in each group, and produced the others as simple tops only, as these serve just as well to show off each distinct mood. The quilters get the freedom to make each design their own by adding borders, sashing or changes of scale to the layout.

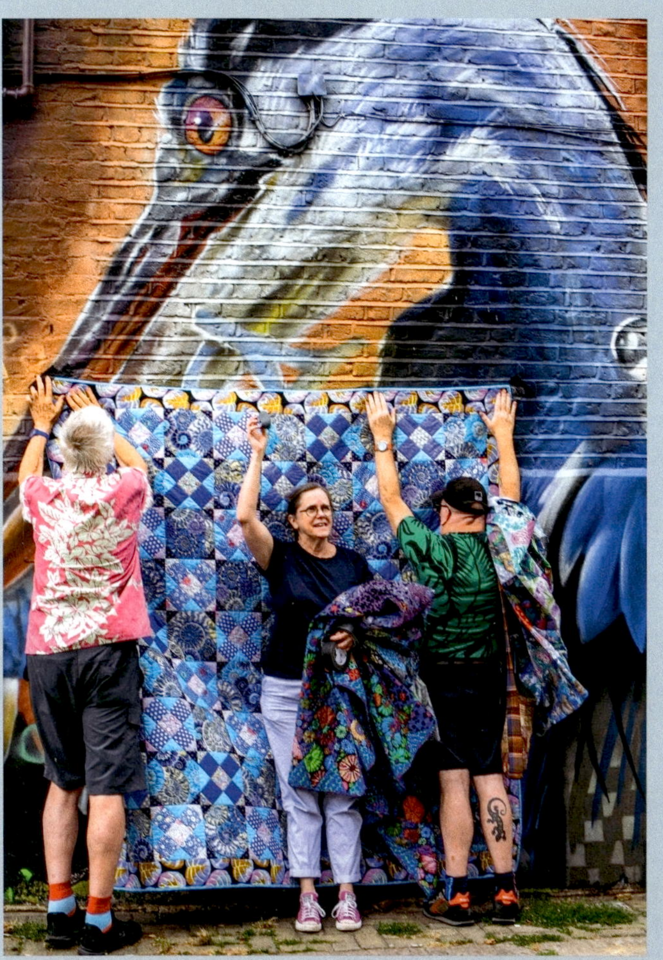

HAWLEY
MEWS. N.W.
THE
REAL ART
OF
STREETART
REDUCED
90%
OFF

Diamonds

The rich but geometric diamond blocks layout varies in its effect according to the fabrics and colours employed, but also in how the diamond blocks themselves are treated.

Bordered Diamonds

In this first group of three quilts, each in a different colourway, I chose to give each diamond quilt a double border. Using feature fabrics and large prints to fussy cut the diamonds themselves and small print fabrics for the borders, I wanted the contrast to draw attention to the individual diamonds. Compare the effect achieved here with the very different effects in the Flowing Diamonds group on pages 16-21.

Bright Bordered Diamonds
by Kaffe Fassett

My first layout for Bordered Diamonds features quite a jolly warm palette. I like the way the predominantly hot reds and pinks work so well with the cooler blues and greens.

Cool Bordered Diamonds
by Kaffe Fassett

This is a block format that I used in my book *Simple Shapes, Spectacular Quilts* to show people how to use my large-scale prints. It's a great way to get the best out of large- and small-scale designs. I've used a cool blue palette here but it's good to see on the following pages the different moods that you can conjure up from the same layout.

Mossy Bordered Diamonds
by Kaffe Fassett

The peaceful waters of the canal which runs through London's Camden Lock Market make such an appropriate setting for this verdant selection of mainly green-based prints. The bright red notes throughout the diamonds and their borders really add a spark to this arrangement.

Flowing Diamonds

In this group of three quilts, the simpler layout (without borders to the diamonds) allows the colour to flow from row to row, creating a harmoniously blended effect. The three colourways in this layout showcase how different each version looks according not only to the choice of colour but also to the scale of the fabric print designs. Large-scale prints work well in this design.

Dark Diamonds
by Kaffe Fassett

One of the benefits of working with the Kaffe Collective large-scale prints is the rich variety you get when the print is repeated across a row so it remains intriguing to the eye. Weren't we lucky to find this wonderful dark mural to show off this rich, dark-toned palette?

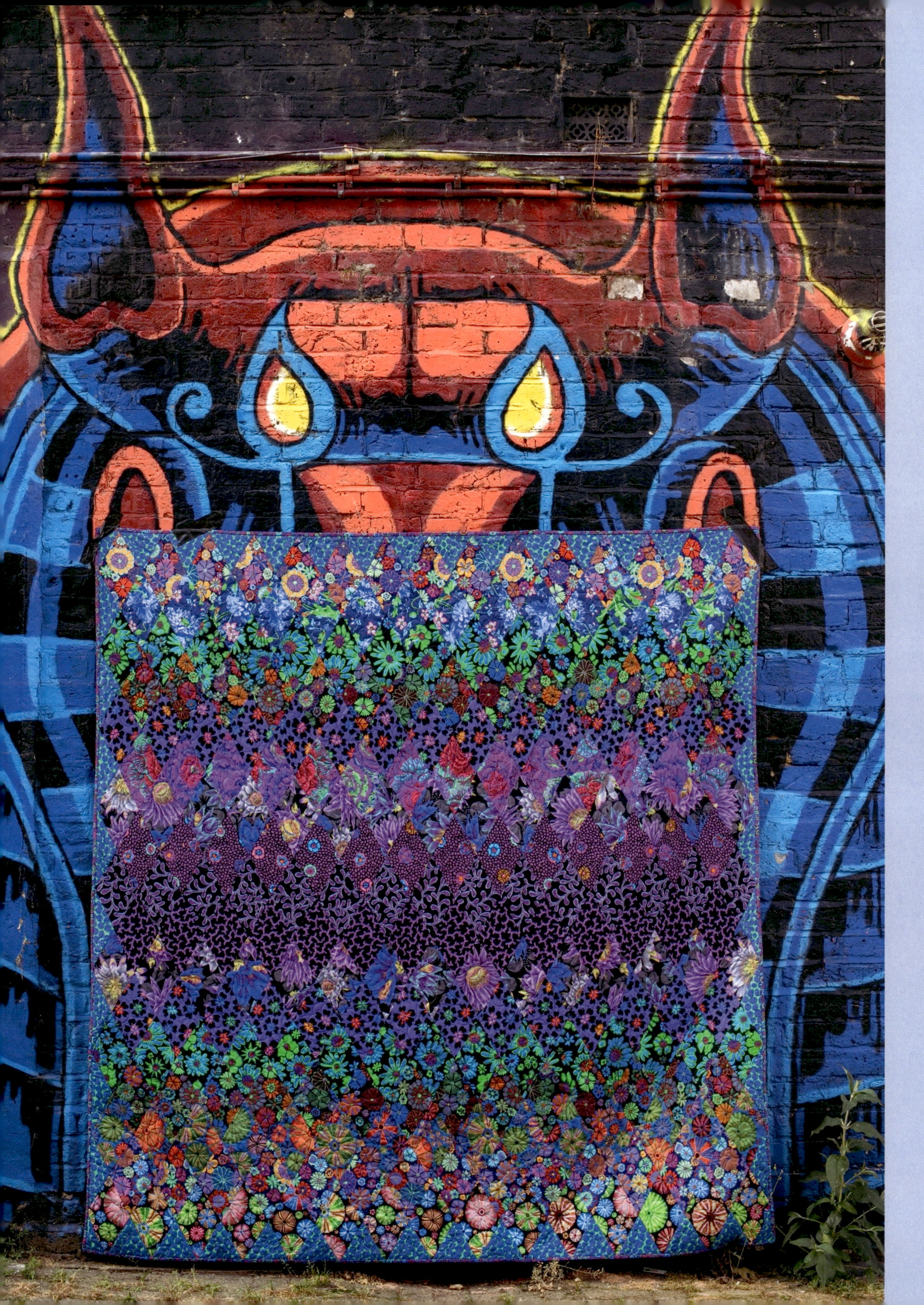

Contrast Diamonds
by Kaffe Fassett

The intricacy of the colour choices in this design was inspired by our recent obsession with black and white. If you start with a black and white theme, it can take added colour very well. I love the high contrasts and how nicely they work with the touches of lime, yellow and pink. This wall at Camden Lock provided a perfect echo of the quilt.

Hot Diamonds
by Kaffe Fassett

The sizzling palette should delight all the lovers of red in this world. It reminds me of a group of Indian women I once saw many years ago in the desert who were waiting for the water truck to arrive. Each and every one of them wore saris in vibrant shades of red, orange and pink. The spectacle seared into my youthful mind's eye and inspired this arrangement.

Roman Tiles

The mosaic-like effect of this block construction, with its central square and opposing triangles, changes in appearance according to the choice of fabric pattern and colour – with contrasts or harmonies – from predominantly subtle and tonal to vibrant and colourful. The theme of the half-square triangle block is carried on into the pieced border. The Roman tiles block lends itself to framing, offering a great opportunity to show off Philip Jacobs' intricate designs for the border.

Contrast Roman Tiles

by Kaffe Fassett

I love this simple graphic layout. I've contrasted icy blues with lush warm prints and was delighted that we found the perfect mural in Camden to make the palette sing. The lime squares in the centre of each block really ping out.

Warm Roman Tiles
by Kaffe Fassett

This is the most complex of our three Roman Tiles tops. It has a mysterious quality as the hot pinks and reds really push against the earthy darker tones.

FLOORS OF

Dark Roman Tiles
by Kaffe Fassett

This striking quilt is a celebration of high contrast. The grey notes in the prints make the three hot colours really pop. The background mural had just the right touches of colour to show it off well.

Medallions

In the group of Medallion quilts that follow, each with a feature fabric in the central panel, the tonal range of each quilt is markedly different, taking its lead from the central print – from the crisp contrasts of the first version to the soft harmonies of the third. The simplicity of the design lets the fabric do the work.

Rich Dark Medallion

by Kaffe Fassett

How powerful the black background prints are in this dramatic quilt! The simple floral border on this lush bouquet of a quilt contrasts with the strong geometric outer border making this quilt a favourite of mine in our collection. The theatrical mural really does it justice.

Rosy Medallion
by Kaffe Fassett

I so love medallion quilts because of the opportunity they give to highlight a large-scale print in the centre. The sharp contrast of the outer border was made stronger by keeping the dark element to a simple two-colour tonal print.

Soft Pastel Medallion
by Liza Prior Lucy

Picking the softest shades in our collection, Liza has created a sweetly gentle baby's quilt – very different from the others in this book. Nestled as it is into the dark foliage of a fig tree at our canal-side location, the quilt's quiet charm can be seen in the best light.

Economy

The popular economy block demonstrates how, in two of the three quilts in this group, an overall colour palette (green or blue) is subtly shifted by using complementary colours as the subsidiary theme – green with mauve or blue with pink. In the third quilt, I ring the changes with a range of largely hot colours: pinks, reds, oranges and mauves. This block lends itself to fussy cutting the prints in the large-scale designs in our collection.

Green Economy
by Kaffe Fassett

What's so exciting for me about this book is the way we get to show how versatile each quilt layout can be. Here I've taken this classic block formula and turned it into a green and pink garden.

Cool Economy
by Kaffe Fassett

This cool version of the economy block layout, in shades of blue, purple and pink, looks really at home against this amazing painted door in Camden.

Hot Economy
by Kaffe Fassett

Here you see the economy layout using a much more jazzed-up approach with volcanic hot shades of red, pink and orange. It shines out against the jumble of colours on a back-alley mural.

Triangles and Stripes

The woven stripes and shot cottons really shimmer in these designs. Using predominantly rich blues, with touches of pinks and purples for one chevron-striped quilt and warm russet tones for the other, shows how to change the mood with subtle gradations of colour in plain fabrics. The easier quilt and the cushions in this group show how striped and plain fabrics can be used to create a different mood in mainly green, rust and blue colourways.

Contrast Chevron Stripes

by Kaffe Fassett

This quilt was inspired by an eye-catching montage of picture frame samples in my local framing shop. It's always a satisfying job to pick the right frame for my latest painting and each time I went there, I knew I should create something from that exciting wall of samples. These layouts were the result.

2
4
6

Russet Chevron Stripes
by Kaffe Fassett

This was the layout to show off many of my hand-woven Indian striped fabrics that have just been brought back into our collection. The rusty wall makes the perfect setting.

Leafy Triangles and Stripes
by Kaffe Fassett

To underline the beautiful tones in each colourway of the exotic stripes in our hand-woven Indian fabric range, I used a leafy shot cotton between each one. I love the way this canal-side setting with its tropical plants resembles the arches of a gothic cathedral.

Triangles and Stripes Cushions

A very simple but effective cushion design, one in warm earthy tones and the other in cool blues, is an ideal way to make use of surplus striped fabrics, especially when given a special border.

Warm Exotic Stripe Cushion

by Kaffe Fassett

These stripes are so versatile, and placing simple triangles together with a border is very effective. Using the narrow stripes in a toning colourway for the border helps to finish it off perfectly.

Cool Wide Stripe Cushion

by Kaffe Fassett

I love the cool blues and greens of the hand-woven stripe for the centre triangles of this cushion, combined with the similar tones of Brandon's Wobble fabric for the border.

Snowballs

In this group of quilts, Liza explores the idea of using an additional block as well as changing the colours in each layout. In her three snowball patchworks, she has demonstrated the block's versatility by alternating it with an additional favourite block in each patchwork. Keeping the main fabric of the snowball block consistent throughout the three designs provides an anchor for the various fabrics in the alternating block. By using the same block in different ways, you can vary the effect with minor changes to the design of the block itself.

Moody Snowball Criss Cross

by Liza Prior Lucy

There is always room for a good blue and white palette in any quilt collection. This fun snowball, which Brandon and I are holding up against a giant bird's-head mural, should fill that slot nicely.

Hot Snowball Circles

by Liza Prior Lucy

Here Liza jumps into high, lively colour and a circular version of her snowball trilogy. The palette of hot pink, orange, red and purple for the snowballs is picked up in the Lotus Leaf fabric border. Doesn't this quilt just zing out against the two funky murals behind it?

Contrast Snowball Stars

by Liza Prior Lucy

This is Liza's dusty palette snowball, in direct contrast to the first quilt in this group. The lower-key shades will appeal to people who find my own colour choices a bit too strong. I like the way the purple/blue tones of the Japanese Chrysanthemum fabric set off the snowballs.

bright bordered diamonds **

Kaffe Fassett

Bordered Diamonds quilts give the opportunity to show off great medium- to large-scale fabric designs, while at the same time selecting some favourite small prints to frame the diamonds. Two further versions are included, each showcasing a different colour palette. The instructions for the alternatives follow the main quilt in terms of construction method but include their own fabric choices. For the backing and bindings of the alternatives, follow the main quilt instructions but choose your own backings and bindings from the lists on page 151.

SIZE OF FINISHED QUILT

83½in x 66½in (212cm x 169cm)

FABRICS

Fabrics have been calculated at a maximum width of 40in (102cm). Fabrics have been given a number – see the Fabric Swatch Diagram on page 56 for details.

Patchwork Fabrics

Diamond fabrics – medium-large scale prints

WOBBLE		
Fabric 1	Pastel	½yd (50cm)
JAPONICA		
Fabric 2	Contrast	½yd (50cm)
PAPAVER		
Fabric 3	Red	½yd (50cm)
JUNGLE		
Fabric 4	Red	½yd (50cm)
LOTUS LEAF		
Fabric 5	Emerald	½yd (50cm)
FOLK FLOWER		
Fabric 6	Pink	½yd (50cm)
Fabric 7	Blue	½yd (50cm)
Fabric 8	Multi	½yd (50cm)
BLOOMERS		
Fabric 9	Green	½yd (50cm)
Fabric 10	Grey	½yd (50cm)
Fabric 11	Lilac	½yd (50cm)
Fabric 12	Orange	½yd (50cm)

Border fabrics – small-scale prints

JUMBLE		
Fabric 13	Yellow	½yd (50cm)
Fabric 14	Rose	½yd (50cm)
Fabric 15	Lime	½yd (50cm)
Fabric 16	Duck Egg	½yd (50cm)
Fabric 17	Bubble Gum	½yd (50cm)
Fabric 18	Turquoise	½yd (50cm)
SNOW FLOWER		
Fabric 19	Black	½yd (50cm)
SPOT		
Fabric 20	Buff	½yd (50cm)
* see also Binding Fabric		
Fabric 21	Toast	½yd (50cm)
GAMEBOARD		
Fabric 22	Purple	½yd (50cm)
Fabric 23	Magenta	1⅛yd (1.1m)
Fabric 24	Pink	½yd (50cm)
Fabric 25	Red	½yd (50cm)
PASHA PAISLEY		
Fabric 26	Pink	½yd (50cm)
Fabric 27	Black	½yd (50cm)

Backing and Binding Fabrics

PEBBLE MOSAIC extra-wide backing		
Fabric 28	Prune	2⅛yd (2m)
SPOT		
Fabric 20	Buff	⅝yd (60cm)
* see also Patchwork Fabrics		

Batting

93in x 76in (236cm x 193cm)

TEMPLATES

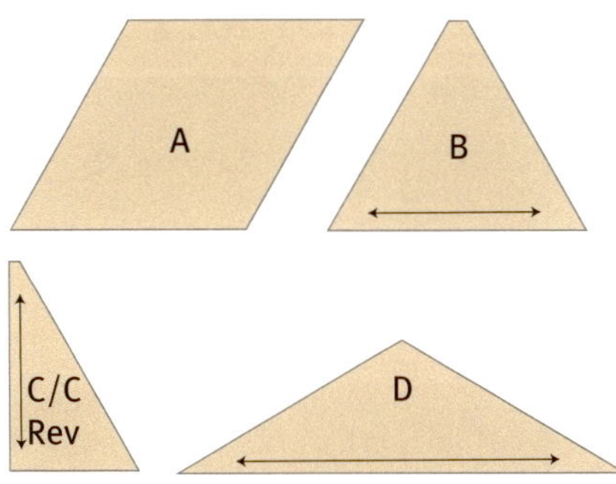

Acrylic templates for 60° diamonds and triangles are available at many patchwork retailers although they are optional as the required templates are printed on pages 142-143.

PATCHES

The patches are 7in (17.8cm) finished 60° diamonds. The diamond borders are made from 1in (2.54cm) finished strips. Bordered diamonds are set in 9 rows of 6 or 7 full diamonds with long half diamonds completing the row edges and short half diamonds filling in the top and bottom, completed with quarter diamonds at the corners.

FABRIC SWATCH DIAGRAM

Patchwork Fabrics

Fabric 1
WOBBLE
Pastel
BM92PT

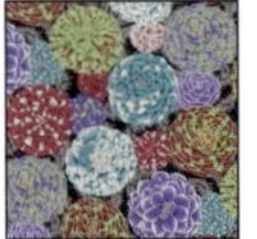
Fabric 2
JAPONICA
Contrast
PJ130CN

Fabric 3
PAPAVER
Red
PJ127RD

Fabric 4
JUNGLE
Red
PJ126RD

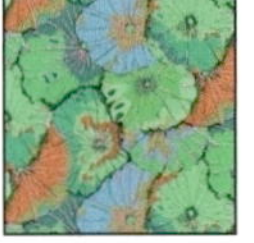
Fabric 5
LOTUS LEAF
Emerald
GP29EM

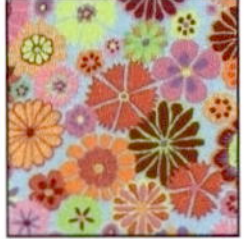
Fabric 6
FOLK FLOWER
Pink
GP204PK

Fabric 7
FOLK FLOWER
Blue
GP204BL

Fabric 8
FOLK FLOWER
Multi
GP204MU

Fabric 9
BLOOMERS
Green
BM93GN

Fabric 10
BLOOMERS
Grey
BM93GY

Fabric 11
BLOOMERS
Lilac
BM93LI

Fabric 12
BLOOMERS
Orange
BM93OR

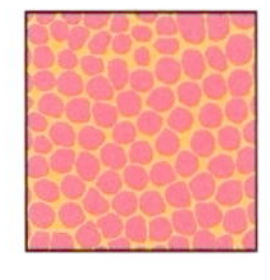
Fabric 13
JUMBLE
Yellow
BM53YE

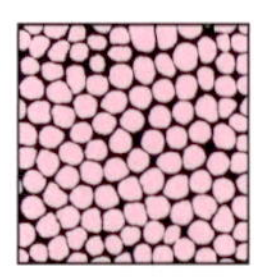
Fabric 14
JUMBLE
Rose
BM53RO

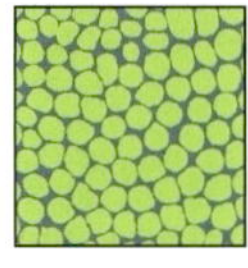
Fabric 15
JUMBLE
Lime
BM53LM

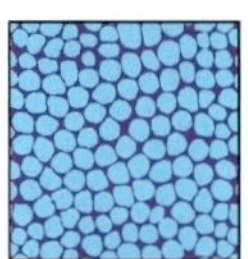
Fabric 16
JUMBLE
Duck Egg
BM53DE

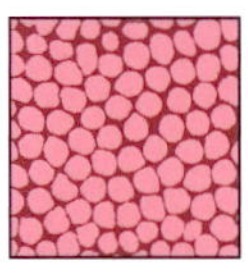
Fabric 17
JUMBLE
Bubblegum
BM53BB

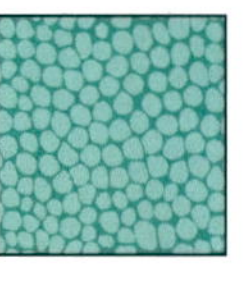
Fabric 18
JUMBLE
Turquoise
BM53TQ

Fabric 19
SNOW FLOWER
Black
BM94BK

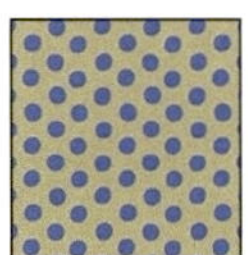
Fabric 20
SPOT
Buff
GP70BF

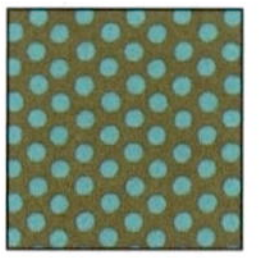
Fabric 21
SPOT
Toast
GP70TT

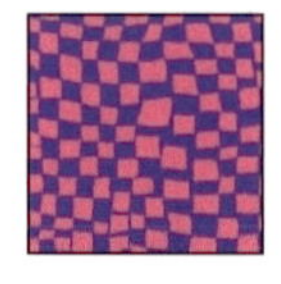
Fabric 22
GAMEBOARD
Purple
BM95PU

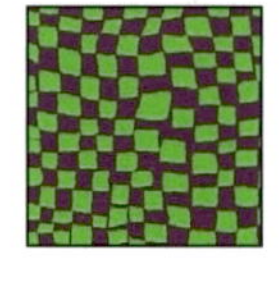
Fabric 23
GAMEBOARD
Magenta
BM95MG

Fabric 24
GAMEBOARD
Pink
BM95PK

Fabric 25
GAMEBOARD
Red
BM95RD

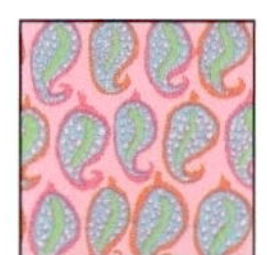
Fabric 26
PASHA PAISLEY
Pink
BM996PK

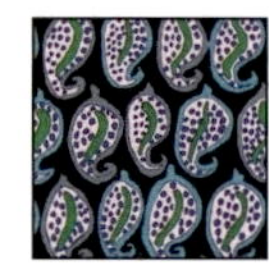
Fabric 27
PASHA PAISLEY
Black
BM996BK

Backing and Binding Fabrics

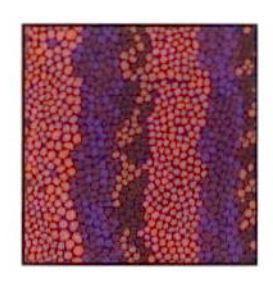
Fabric 28
PEBBLE MOSAIC
Prune
QM04PV

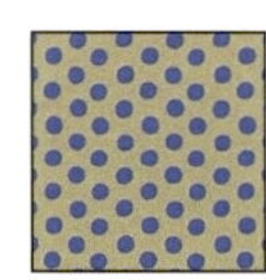
Fabric 20
SPOT
Buff
GP70BF

CUTTING OUT

Fabric is cut across the width unless otherwise stated. When cutting different pieces from the same fabric, always cut the larger pieces first. For best results, use spray starch before cutting.

Diamonds

You will need 59 whole diamonds, 8 long half diamonds, 12 short half diamonds and 2 each of the quarter diamond and reverse quarter diamond. Most patches are cut from strips cut across the width of fabric, but some are fussy cut to centre a bloom within the diamond. We have provided the number of diamonds cut from each fabric to follow the layout in the book exactly, however if you prefer to use more or less of some fabrics, there is extra fabric included for this.

CUTTING DIAGRAM

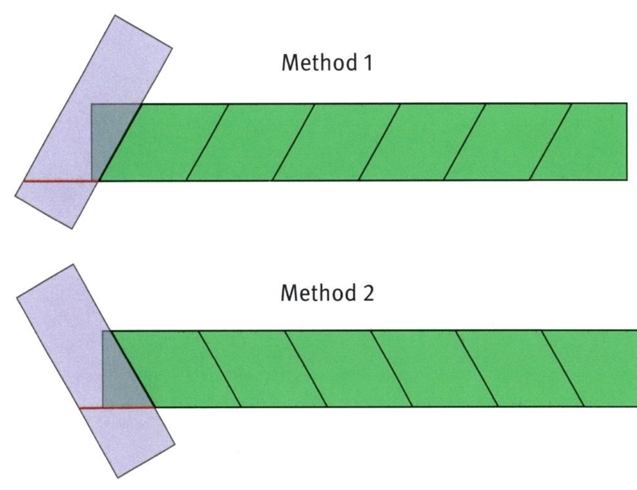

Fussy-cut Diamonds

Using card/plastic templates made from the templates on pages 142-143, fussy cut Template A diamonds, Template B short half diamonds and Template C/C Reverse quarter diamonds, centring a bloom approximately within each patch, from fabrics as follows:

Fabric 2 6 full diamonds, 2 short half diamonds, 1 reverse quarter diamond;
Fabric 3 5 full diamonds, 1 short half diamond.

Strip-cut Diamonds

Cut 2 strips $6^{1}/_{2}$in (16.51cm) wide from each of **Fabrics 1, 4, 5, 6, 7, 8, 9, 10, 11** and **12**. Referring to the Cutting Diagram, cross cut Template A diamonds. Alternate between cutting methods 1 and 2 so there is a good mix cut using each method. Sewing a grain-cut edge to a bias-cut edge prevents stretching. Each strip will yield at least 4 full diamonds, leaving enough at the strip ends to cut the required Template B short half diamonds and Template C/C Reverse quarter diamonds. Cut patches from fabrics as follows:

Fabric 1 5 diamonds;
Fabric 4 5 diamonds, 1 short half diamond;
Fabric 5 5 diamonds, 2 short half diamonds;
Fabric 6 4 full diamonds, 1 short half diamond;
Fabric 7 5 full diamonds, 1 quarter diamond;
Fabric 8 5 full diamonds, 1 short half diamond, 1 quarter diamond;
Fabric 9 5 full diamonds;
Fabric 10 5 full diamonds;
Fabric 11 5 full diamonds;
Fabric 12 4 full diamonds, 3 short half diamonds, 1 reverse quarter diamond.

Long Half Diamonds

From the remaining fabric, use Template D to cut long half diamonds, making sure the long edge runs along the grain. These edges will complete rows and form the edges of the quilt top. Cut a long half diamond from each of **Fabrics 2, 4, 5, 7, 9, 10, 11** and **12**.

Outer Border

From **Fabric 23** cut 8 strips $2^{1}/_{2}$in (6.4cm) wide. Join strips end to end using $^{1}/_{4}$in (6mm) seams, and press seams open. From the length cut:
2 pieces $80^{1}/_{2}$in x $2^{1}/_{2}$in (204.5cm x 6.4cm) for the side borders;
2 pieces $67^{1}/_{2}$in x $2^{1}/_{2}$in (171.5cm x 6.4cm) for the top and bottom borders.

Diamond Borders

Cut strips $1^{1}/_{2}$in (3.8cm) wide to create diamond borders. There is ample fabric allowed to cut 8 sets of borders from each border fabric. From each of **Fabrics 13-27** cut up to 10 strips $1^{1}/_{2}$in (3.8cm) wide and cross cut the border pieces as follows:
Each full diamond: 1 piece 9in (23cm) long, 2 pieces 11in (28cm) long and 1 piece 12in (30.5cm) long.
Each short half diamond: 1 piece 9in (23cm) long and 1 piece 11in (28cm) long.
Each long half diamond: 1 piece 11in (28cm) long and 1 piece 12in (30.5cm) long.
Each quarter diamond for the corners: 1 piece 9in (23cm) long.

Backing

Trim **Fabric 28** backing fabric to 93in x 76in (236cm x 193cm).

Binding

From **Fabric 20** cut 8 strips $2^{1}/_{2}$in (6.4cm) wide. Remove selvedges and sew end to end with 45° seams (see page 149).

WHOLE DIAMOND BLOCK ASSEMBLY DIAGRAM

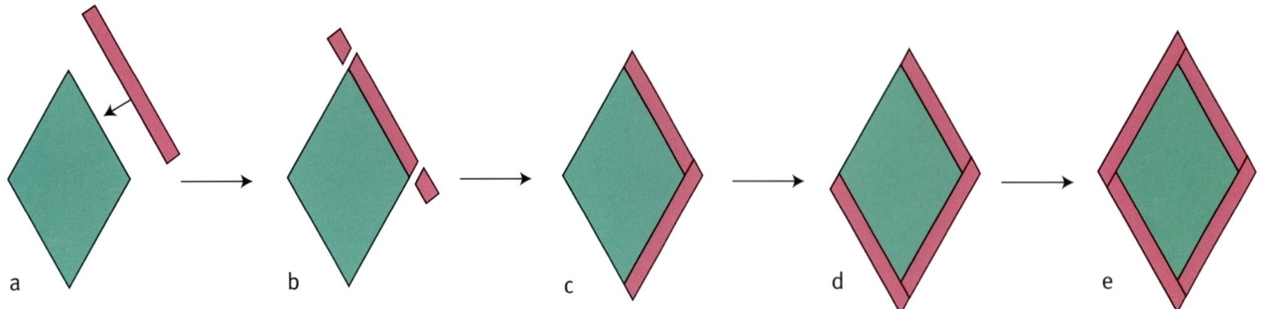

PARTIAL DIAMOND BLOCK ASSEMBLY DIAGRAMS

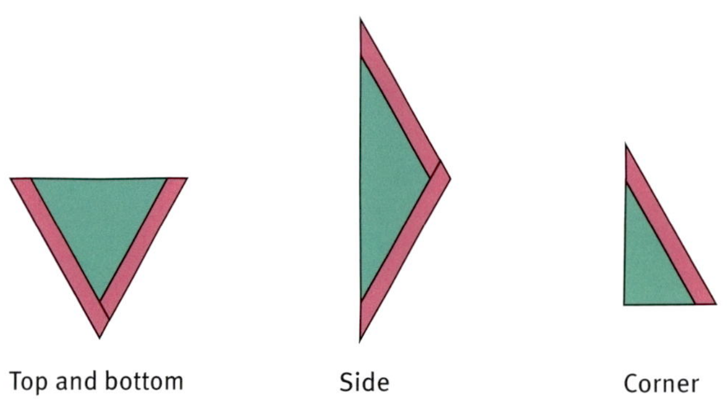

MAKING THE QUILT

Using a design wall will help to place patches in the required layout.
Use ¼in (6mm) seams throughout.

Making the Blocks

Referring to the Block Assembly Diagram, choose a border fabric that contrasts well for each diamond patch. Follow steps **a** to **e** to sew a border to each diamond, using border lengths as shown below, pressing and trimming each side in turn.

a. Sew a 9in (23cm) strip to the edge of the upper right side of the diamond.
b. Press and trim off the ends of the strip so it continues the line of the diamond.
c. Sew an 11in (28cm) strip to the bottom right side in the same way, press and trim.
d. Sew an 11in (28cm) strip to the bottom left side, press and trim.
e. Sew a 12in (30.5cm) strip to the top left side, press and trim.

Referring to the Partial Diamond Block Assembly Diagrams, make 12 top and bottom short half-diamond blocks in the same way using a 9in (23cm) strip and an 11in (28cm) strip, ensuring the straight grain side is open, not bordered.
Make 8 long half-diamond blocks for the sides, using an 11in (28cm) strip and a 12in (30.5cm) strip for each, leaving the long edge open, not bordered.
Make 4 quarter-diamond blocks for the corners using a 12in (30.5cm) strip on the long diagonal side.

Quilt Assembly

Referring to the Quilt Assembly Diagram and the quilt photograph, arrange the blocks and partial blocks in 9 alternating rows of 7 or 6 diamonds. Fabric numbers for the diamonds have been included on the diagram should you wish to copy the layout exactly. Begin by laying out the 59 whole diamonds, then add partial diamonds to complete the layout.
Sew the diamonds together in diagonal rows, pressing seams in opposite directions on alternate rows – odd rows to the left, even rows to the right – to allow the finished seams to lie flat. Sew the diagonal rows together taking care to align crossing seams and points.

Border

Pin (to prevent stretching the borders) and sew the longer side borders to the centre, press seams towards the border, then pin and sew the top and bottom borders to the centre to complete the quilt top.

FINISHING THE QUILT

Press the quilt top. Layer the quilt top, batting and backing, and baste together (see page 148).
Quilt as desired.
Trim the quilt edges and attach the binding (see page 149).

QUILT ASSEMBLY DIAGRAM

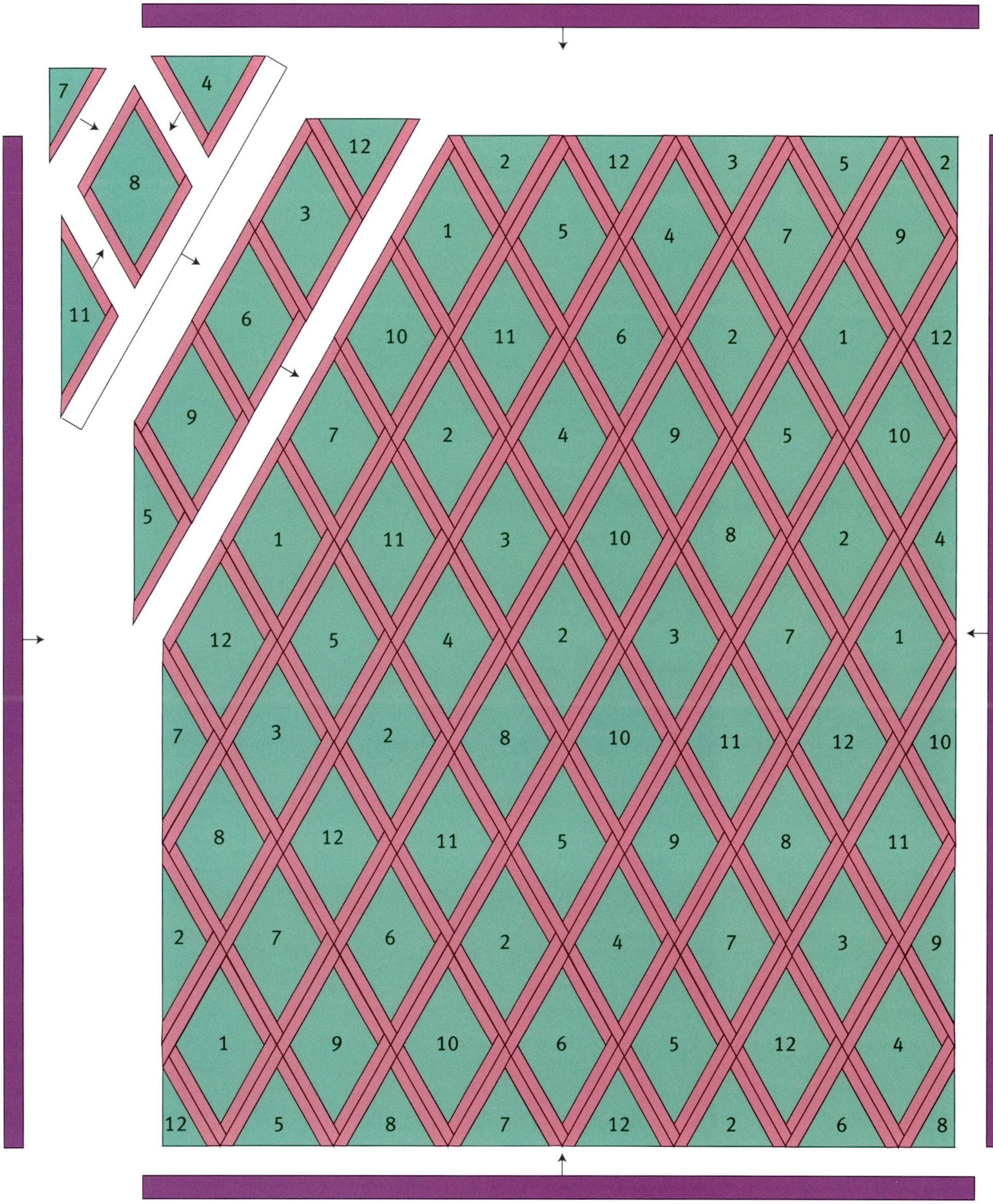

Fabric 1, 2, 3, 4, 5, 6, 7, 8, 9, 10, 11, 12

Fabric 13, 14, 15, 16, 17, 18, 19, 20, 21, 22, 23, 24, 25, 26, 27

Fabric 23

cool bordered diamonds **

Kaffe Fassett

This version of Bordered Diamonds features some of our beautiful blue designs, both for the large-scale diamonds and the small-scale borders. The instruction method is the same as that for the *Bright Bordered Diamonds* quilt, but with different fabrics. Follow the *Bright Bordered Diamonds* instructions on pages 55-59 but use the fabrics as listed here and shown in the Quilt Assembly Diagram.

SIZE OF FINISHED QUILT

83½in x 66½in (212cm x 169cm)

Patchwork Fabrics

Diamond fabrics – medium-large scale prints

WOBBLE

Fabric 1	Blue	½yd (50cm)

BLOOMERS

Fabric 2	Cobalt	½yd (50cm)

URCHIN

Fabric 3	Blue	½yd (50cm)
Fabric 4	Multi	½yd (50cm)

JUNGLE

Fabric 5	Neutral	½yd (50cm)

PAPAVER

Fabric 6	Blue	½yd (50cm)
Fabric 7	Green	½yd (50cm)

AMMONITES

Fabric 8	Blue	½yd (50cm)

JAPONICA

Fabric 9	Blue	½yd (50cm)
Fabric 10	Pastel	½yd (50cm)

Border fabrics – small-scale prints

SPOT

Fabric 11	Black	½yd (50cm)
Fabric 12	Peacock	½yd (50cm)
Fabric 13	Spring	½yd (50cm)
Fabric 14	Indigo	1⅛yd (1.1m)
Fabric 15	Green	½yd (50cm)

GAMEBOARD

Fabric 16	Purple	1½yd (50cm)

JUMBLE

Fabric 17	Blue	½yd (50cm)
Fabric 18	Purple	½yd (50cm)
Fabric 19	Ocean	½yd (50cm)
Fabric 20	Duck Egg	½yd (50cm)
Fabric 21	Cobalt	½yd (50cm)

INSTRUCTIONS

Follow the cutting and making instructions on pages 55-59 and simply replace the same-titled sections with the corresponding sections below.

FABRIC SWATCH DIAGRAM

Patchwork Fabrics

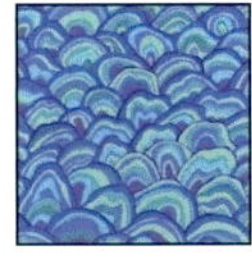

Fabric 1
WOBBLE
Blue
BM92BL

Fabric 2
BLOOMERS
Cobalt
BM93CB

Fabric 3
URCHIN
Blue
PJ125BL

Fabric 4
URCHIN
Multi
PJ125MU

Fabric 5
JUNGLE
Neutral
PJ126NE

Fabric 6
PAPAVER
Blue
PJ127BL

Fabric 7
PAPAVER
Green
PJ127GN

Fabric 8
AMMONITES
Blue
PJ128BL

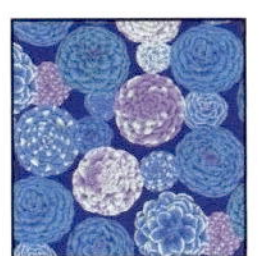

Fabric 9
JAPONICA
Blue
PJ130BL

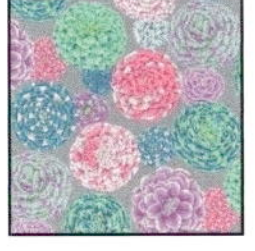

Fabric 10
JAPONICA
Pastel
PJ130PT

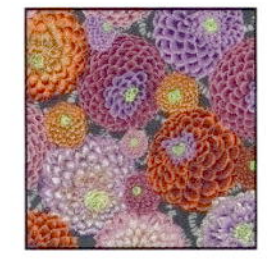

Fabric 11
SPOT
Black
GP70BK

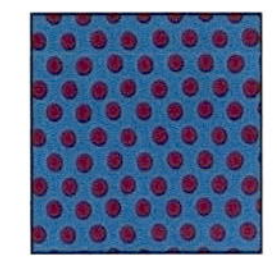

Fabric 12
SPOT
Peacock
GP70PC

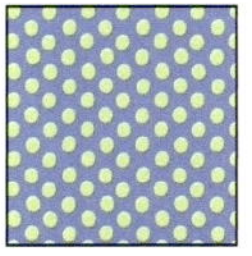

Fabric 13
SPOT
Spring
GP70SP

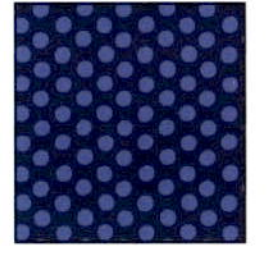

Fabric 14
SPOT
Indigo
GP70IN

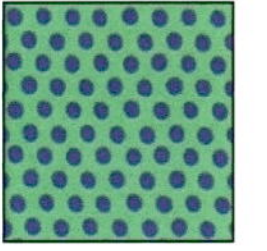

Fabric 15
SPOT
Green
GP70GN

Fabric 16
GAMEBOARD
Purple
BM95PU

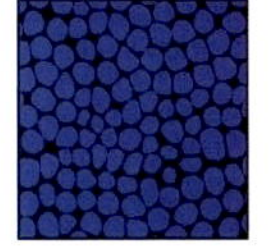

Fabric 17
JUMBLE
Blue
BM53BL

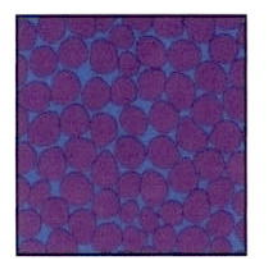

Fabric 18
JUMBLE
Purple
BM53PU

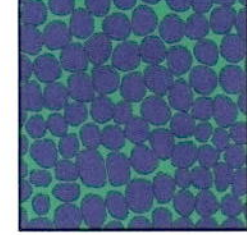

Fabric 19
JUMBLE
Ocean
BM53ON

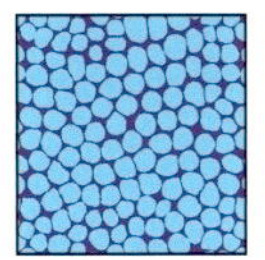

Fabric 20
JUMBLE
Duck Egg
BM53DE

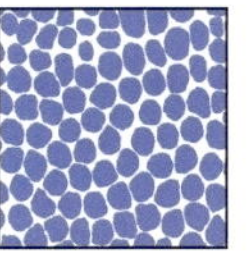

Fabric 21
JUMBLE
Cobalt
BM53CB

Fussy-cut Diamonds

Using card/plastic templates made from the templates on pages 142-143, fussy cut Template A diamonds, Template B short half diamonds and Template C/C Reverse quarter diamonds, centring a bloom approximately within each patch, from fabrics as follows:

Fabric 6 6 full diamonds, 1 short half diamond, 1 reverse quarter diamond;
Fabric 7 6 full diamonds, 1 short half diamond;
Fabric 9 5 full diamonds, 1 short half diamond;
Fabric 10 5 full diamonds, 1 short half diamond, 1 quarter diamond.

Strip-cut Diamonds

Cut 2 strips 6½in (16.51cm) wide from each of **Fabrics 1, 2, 3, 4, 5** and **8**. Referring to the Cutting Diagram on page 57, cross cut Template A diamonds. Alternate between cutting methods 1 and 2 to give a good mix of diamonds cut using each method. Sewing a grain-cut edge to a bias-cut edge prevents stretching. Each strip will yield at least 4 full diamonds, leaving enough at the strip ends to cut the required Template B short half diamonds and Template C/C Reverse quarter diamonds. Cut patches from fabrics as follows:

Fabric 1 6 diamonds, 2 short half diamonds, 1 reverse quarter diamond;
Fabric 2 6 diamonds, 2 short half diamonds, 1 quarter diamond;
Fabric 3 7 diamonds, 1 short half diamond;
Fabric 4 6 diamonds, 1 short half diamond;
Fabric 5 6 diamonds, 1 short half diamond;
Fabric 8 6 diamonds, 1 short half diamond.

Long Half Diamonds

From the remaining fabric, use Template D to cut long half diamonds, making sure the long edge runs along the grain. These edges will complete rows and form the edges of the quilt top. Cut long half diamonds from fabrics as follows:

Fabric 1 1 long half diamond;
Fabric 2 1 long half diamond;
Fabric 3 1 long half diamond;
Fabric 4 1 long half diamond;
Fabric 5 2 long half diamonds;
Fabric 8 1 long half diamond;
Fabric 10 1 long half diamond.

Outer Border

From **Fabric 14** cut 8 strips 2½in (6.4cm) wide. Join strips end to end using ¼in (6mm) seams, and press seams open. From the length, cut:
2 pieces 80½in x 2½in (204.5cm x 6.4cm) for the side borders;
2 pieces 67½in x 2½in (171.5cm x 6.4cm) for the top and bottom borders.

Diamond Borders

Cut strips 1½in (3.8cm) wide to create diamond borders. There is ample fabric to cut 8 sets of borders from each border fabric. From each of **Fabrics 11-21** cut up to 10 strips 1½in (3.8cm) wide and cross cut the border pieces as follows:
Each full diamond: 1 piece 9in (23cm) long, 2 pieces 11in (28cm) long and 1 piece 12in (30.5cm) long.
Each short half diamond: 1 piece 9in (23cm) long and 1 piece 11in (28cm) long.
Each long half diamond: 1 piece 11in (28cm) long and 1 piece 12in (30.5cm) long.
Each quarter diamond for the corners: 1 piece 9in (23cm) long.

Border

Pin (to prevent stretching the borders) and sew the longer **Fabric 14** side borders to the centre, press seams towards the border, then pin and sew the top and bottom borders to the centre.

FINISHING THE QUILT

This patchwork has been finished as a patchwork top. To prevent fraying, sew a double hem around the outer edge of the border to complete the top.
If you prefer to quilt your patchwork, cut batting and backing 8in (20.3cm) larger than the quilt top. Layer the quilt top, batting and backing, and baste together (see page 148).
Quilt as desired.
Trim the quilt edges and attach the binding (see page 149).

QUILT ASSEMBLY DIAGRAM

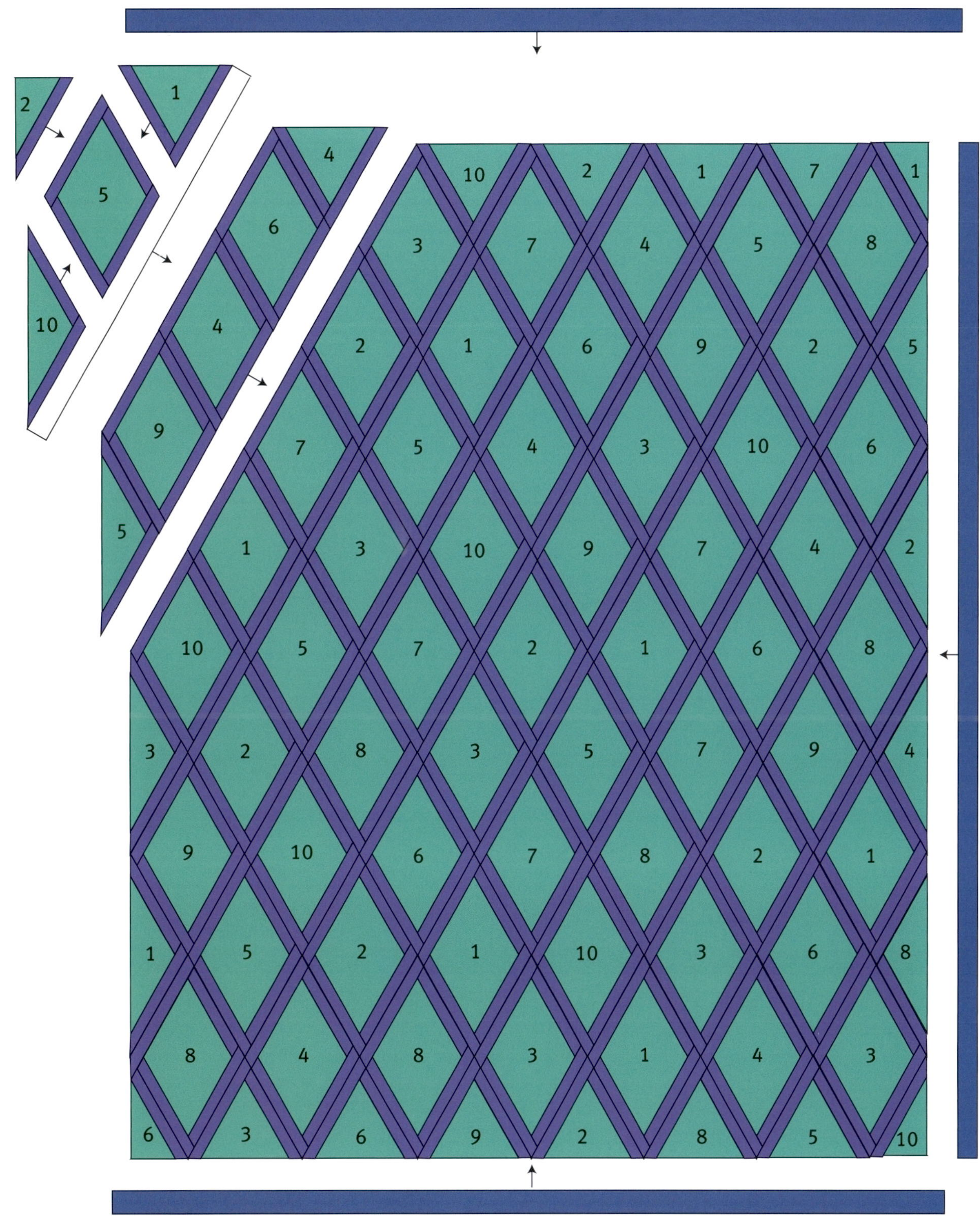

Fabric 1, 2, 3, 4, 5, 6, 7, 8, 9, 10

Fabric 11, 12, 13, 14, 15, 16, 17, 18, 19, 20, 21

Fabric 14

mossy bordered diamonds **

Kaffe Fassett

In this version, a green medley of our larger-scale fabric designs is used for the diamonds with a lively selection of our small prints old and new for the borders. Follow the *Bright Bordered Diamonds* instructions on pages 55-59 but use the fabrics as listed here and shown in the Quilt Assembly Diagram.

SIZE OF FINISHED QUILT
83½in x 66½in (212cm x 169cm)

Patchwork Fabrics
Diamond fabrics – medium-large scale prints

WOBBLE
Fabric 1 Green ½yd (50cm)
BLOOMERS
Fabric 2 Black ½yd (50cm)
LOTUS LEAF
Fabric 3 Emerald ½yd (50cm)
FOLK FLOWER
Fabric 4 Dark ½yd (50cm)
URCHIN
Fabric 5 Dark ½yd (50cm)
AMMONITES
Fabric 6 Dark ½yd (50cm)
Fabric 7 Neutral ⅜yd (40cm)
FITTONIA
Fabric 8 Green ½yd (50cm)
JAPONICA
Fabric 9 Dark ½yd (50cm)
Fabric 10 Green ½yd (50cm)

Border fabrics – small-scale prints

FITTONIA
Fabric 11 Red ½yd (50cm)
REFLECTIONS
Fabric 12 Green ½yd (50cm)
Fabric 13 Brown ½yd (50cm)
Fabric 14 Black ½yd (50cm)
Fabric 15 Moss ½yd (50cm)
GAMEBOARD
Fabric 16 Magenta ½yd (50cm)
SPOT
Fabric 17 Violet 1⅛yd (1.1m)
Fabric 18 Toast ½yd (50cm)
Fabric 19 Merlot ½yd (50cm)
PAPERWEIGHT
Fabric 20 Gypsy ½yd (50cm)
Fabric 21 Emerald ½yd (50cm)
ROMAN GLASS
Fabric 22 Emerald ½yd (50cm)

FABRIC SWATCH DIAGRAM

Patchwork Fabrics

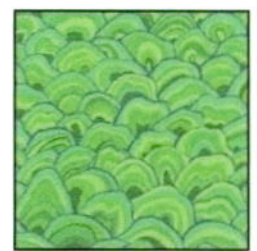
Fabric 1
WOBBLE
Green
BM92GN

Fabric 2
BLOOMERS
Black
BM93BK

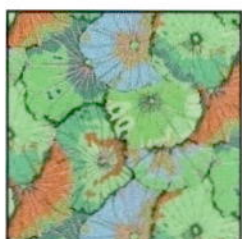
Fabric 3
LOTUS LEAF
Emerald
GP29EM

Fabric 4
FOLK FLOWER
Dark
GP204DK

Fabric 5
URCHIN
Dark
PJ125DK

Fabric 6
AMMONITES
Dark
PJ128DK

Fabric 7
AMMONITES
Neutral
PJ128NE

Fabric 8
FITTONIA
Green
PJ129GN

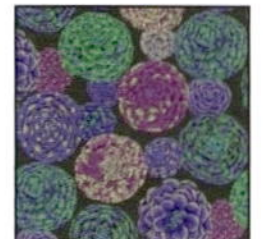
Fabric 9
JAPONICA
Dark
PJ130DK

Fabric 10
JAPONICA
Green
PJ130GN

Fabric 11
FITTONIA
Red
PJ129RD

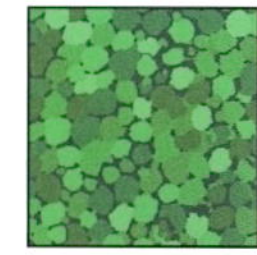
Fabric 12
REFLECTIONS
Green
BM87GN

Fabric 13
REFLECTIONS
Brown
BM87BR

Fabric 14
REFLECTIONS
Black
BM87BK

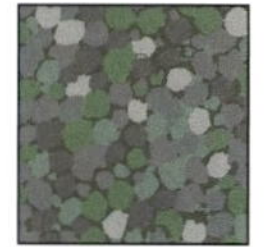
Fabric 15
REFLECTIONS
Moss
BM87MS

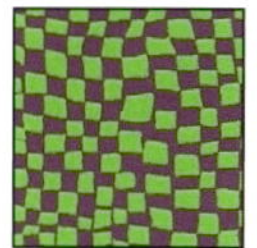
Fabric 16
GAMEBOARD
Magenta
BM95MG

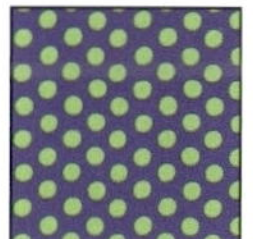
Fabric 17
SPOT
Violet
GP70VI

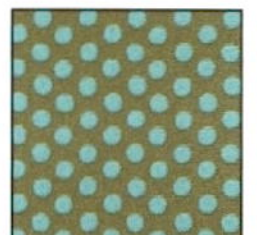
Fabric 18
SPOT
Toast
GP70TT

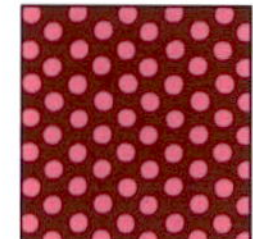
Fabric 19
SPOT
Merlot
GP70MH

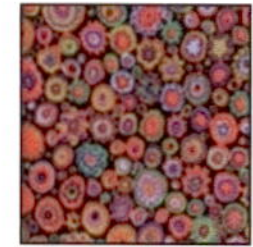
Fabric 20
PAPERWEIGHT
Gypsy
GP20GS

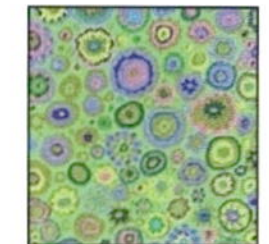
Fabric 21
PAPERWEIGHT
Emerald
GP20EM

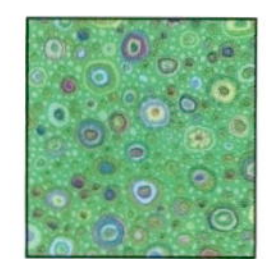
Fabric 22
ROMAN GLASS
Emerald
GP01EM

INSTRUCTIONS

Follow the cutting and making instructions on pages 55-59 and simply replace the same-titled sections with the corresponding sections below.

Fussy-cut Diamonds

Using card/plastic templates made from the templates on pages 142-143, fussy cut Template A diamonds, Template B short half diamonds and Template C/C Reverse quarter diamonds, centring a bloom approximately within each patch, from fabrics as follows:

Fabric 9 5 full diamonds;
Fabric 10 3 full diamonds, 1 short half diamond, 1 reverse quarter diamond.

Strip-cut Diamonds

Cut 2 strips 6½in (16.51cm) wide from each of **Fabrics 1, 2, 3, 4, 5, 6, 7** and **8**. Referring to the Cutting Diagram on page 57, cross cut Template A diamonds. Alternate between cutting methods 1 and 2 to give a good mix of diamonds cut using each method. Sewing a grain-cut edge to a bias-cut edge prevents stretching. Each strip will yield at least 4 full diamonds, leaving enough at the strip ends to cut the required Template B short half diamonds and Template C/C Reverse quarter diamonds. Cut patches from fabrics as follows:

Fabric 1 4 diamonds, 2 short half diamonds;
Fabric 2 7 diamonds, 2 short half diamonds;
Fabric 3 8 diamonds, 1 quarter diamond;
Fabric 4 8 diamonds, 2 short half diamonds;
Fabric 5 9 diamonds, 1 reverse quarter diamond;
Fabric 6 6 full diamonds, 2 short half diamonds;
Fabric 7 3 full diamonds, 1 short half diamond;
Fabric 8 6 full diamonds, 2 short half diamond, 1 quarter diamond.

Long Half Diamonds

From the remaining fabric, use Template D to cut long half diamonds, making sure the long edge runs along the grain. These edges will complete rows and form the edges of the quilt top. Cut a long half diamond from each of **Fabrics 1, 2, 3, 4, 5, 7, 8** and **10**.

Outer Border

From **Fabric 17** cut 8 strips 2½in (6.4cm) wide. Join strips end to end using ¼in (6mm) seams, and press seams open. From the length cut:
2 pieces 80½in x 2½in (204.5cm x 6.4cm) for the side borders;
2 pieces 67½in x 2½in (171.5cm x 6.4cm) for the top and bottom borders.

Diamond Borders

Cut strips 1½in (3.8cm) wide to create diamond borders. There is ample fabric to cut 8 sets of borders from each border fabric. From each of **Fabrics 11-22** cut up to 10 strips 1½in (3.8cm) wide and cross cut the border pieces as follows:
Each full diamond: 1 piece 9in (23cm) long, 2 pieces 11in (28cm) long and 1 piece 12in (30.5cm) long.
Each short half diamond: 1 piece 9in (23cm) long and 1 piece 11in (28cm) long.
Each long half diamond: 1 piece 11in (28cm) long and 1 piece 12in (30.5cm) long.
Each quarter diamond for the corners: 1 piece 9in (23cm) long.

Border

Pin (to prevent stretching the borders) and sew the longer **Fabric 17** side borders to the centre, press seams towards the border, then pin and sew the top and bottom borders to the centre.

FINISHING THE QUILT

This patchwork has been finished as a patchwork top. To prevent fraying, sew a double hem around the outer edge of the border to complete the top.
If you prefer to quilt your patchwork, cut batting and backing 8in (20.3cm) larger than the quilt top. Layer the quilt top, batting and backing, and baste together (see page 148).
Quilt as desired.
Trim the quilt edges and attach the binding (see page 149).

QUILT ASSEMBLY DIAGRAM

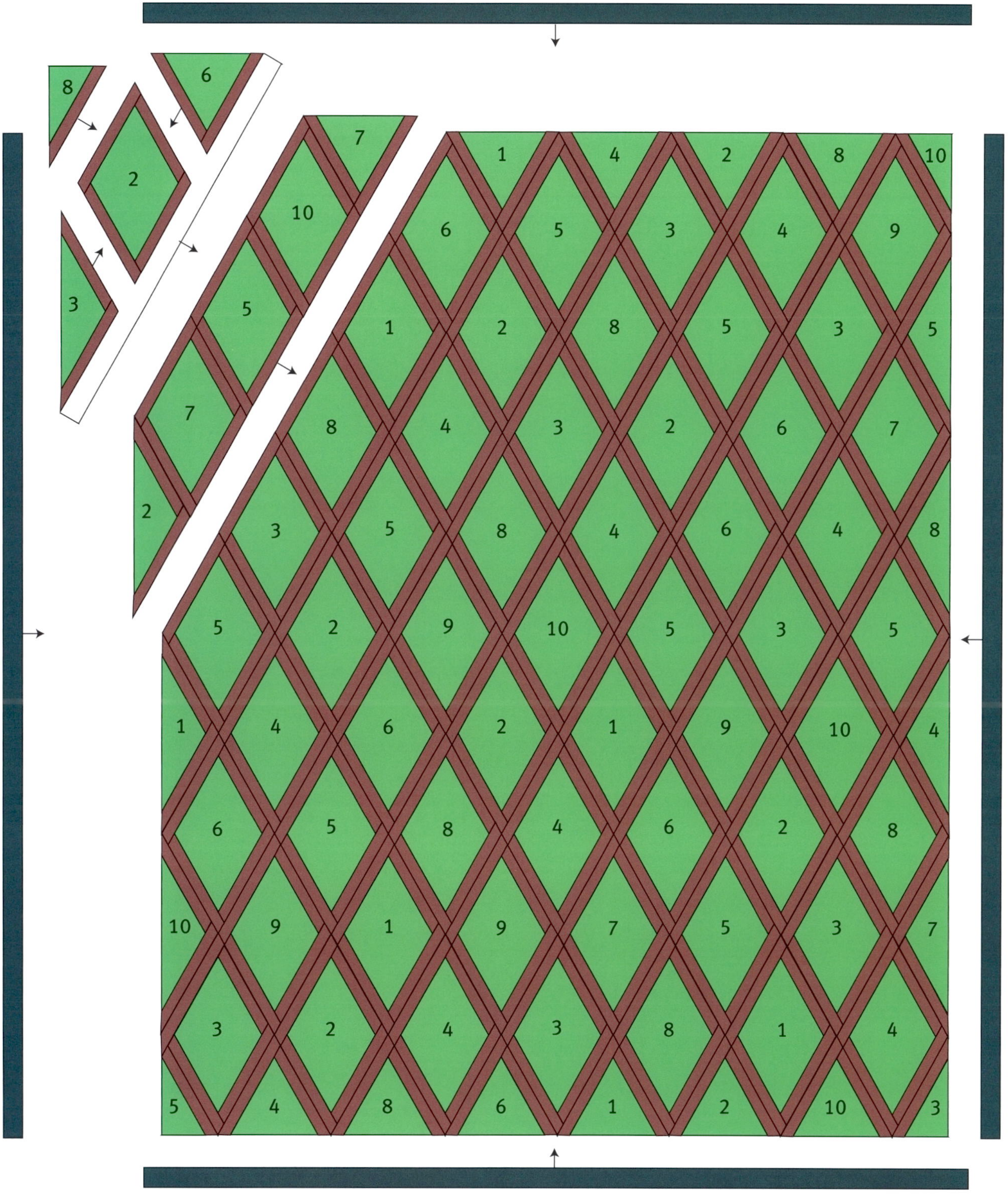

Fabric 1, 2, 3, 4, 5, 6, 7, 8, 9, 10

Fabric 11, 12, 13, 14, 15, 16, 17, 18, 19, 20, 21, 22

Fabric 17

dark diamonds **

Kaffe Fassett

Diamonds, in this case 60° diamonds, set in horizontal rows in different prints, merge and blend together to give a delightful ombre effect. This rich purple patchwork melds blues and greens into purple and back again, with two further versions each showcasing a different colour palette. The instructions for the alternatives follow the main quilt construction method but include their own fabric choices. For the backing and bindings of the alternatives, follow the main quilt instructions but choose your own backings and bindings from the lists on page 151.

SIZE OF FINISHED QUILT

81in x 79in (206cm x 201cm)

FABRICS

Fabrics have been calculated at a maximum width of 40in (102cm) and cut across the width, unless otherwise stated. Fabrics have been given a number – see the Fabric Swatch Diagram for details.

Patchwork Fabrics

JUMBLE

Fabric 1	Ocean	7/8yd (85cm)

URCHIN

Fabric 2	Multi	1/2yd (50cm)
Fabric 3	Dark	1/2yd (50cm)

FOLK FLOWER

Fabric 4	Purple	3/4yd (70cm)
Fabric 5	Dark	3/4yd (70cm)

BLOOMERS

Fabric 6	Black	3/4yd (70cm)

PETALS

Fabric 7	Purple	3/4yd (70cm)

CACTUS FLOWER

Fabric 8	Black	3/4yd (70cm)

CORAL

Fabric 9	Purple	1/2yd (50cm)

TWIG

Fabric 10	Black	1/2yd (50cm)

GUINEA FLOWER

Fabric 11	Purple	1/2yd (50cm)

BRASSICA

Fabric 12	Purple	1/2yd (50cm)

PAPAVER

Fabric 13	Blue	1/2yd (50cm)

FABRIC SWATCH DIAGRAM

Patchwork Fabrics

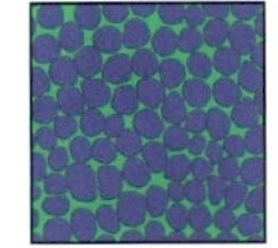

Fabric 1
JUMBLE
Ocean
BM53ON

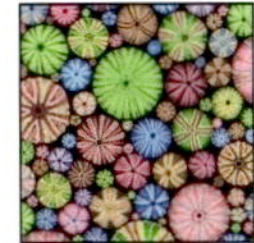

Fabric 2
URCHIN
Multi
PJ125MU

Fabric 3
URCHIN
Dark
PJ125DK

Fabric 4
FOLK FLOWER
Purple
GP204PU

Fabric 5
FOLK FLOWER
Dark
GP204DK

Fabric 6
BLOOMERS
Black
BM93BK

Fabric 7
PETALS
Purple
GP201PU

Fabric 8
CACTUS FLOWER
Black
PJ96BK

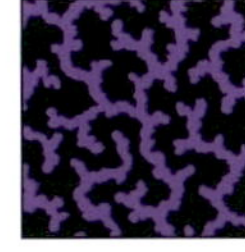

Fabric 9
CORAL
Purple
PJ04PU

Fabric 10
TWIG
Black
GP196BK

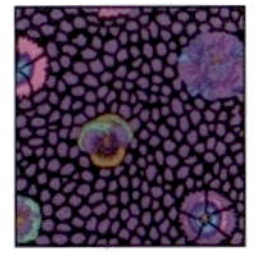

Fabric 11
GUINEA FLOWER
Purple
GP59PU

Fabric 12
BRASSICA
Purple
PJ51PU

Fabric 13
PAPAVER
Blue
PJ127BL

Backing and Binding Fabrics

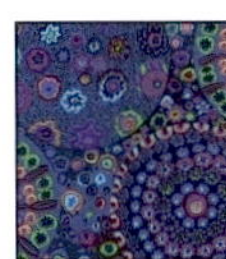

Fabric 14
MILLEFIORE
Blue
QB06BL

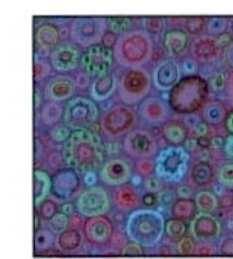

Fabric 15
PAPERWEIGHT
Purple
GP20PU

Backing and Binding Fabrics

MILLEFIORE extra-wide backing

Fabric 14	Blue	2 1/2yd (2.3m)

PAPERWEIGHT

Fabric 15	Purple	3/4yd (70cm)

Batting

89in x 87in (226cm x 221cm)

TEMPLATES

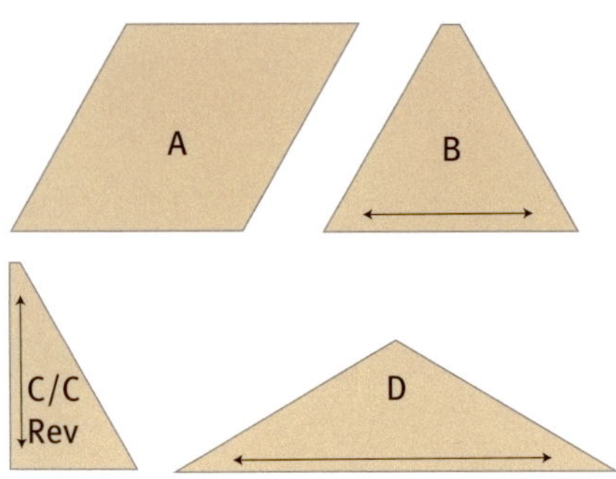

CUTTING DIAGRAM

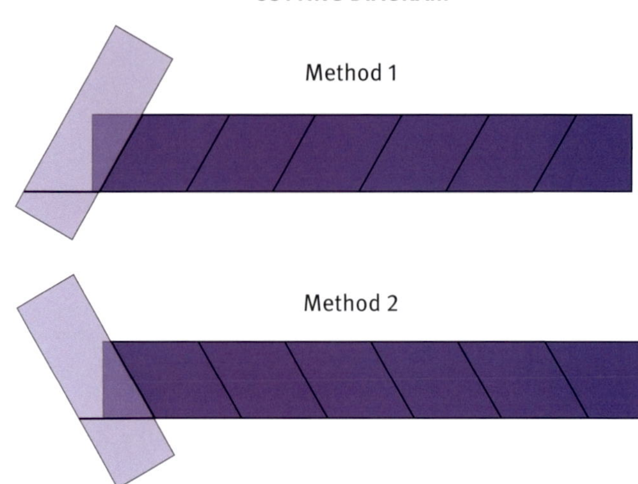

Patches

The quilt is made of 60° diamond and triangle patches that can be cut from strips using a 60° ruler or by using Templates A, B, C/C Reverse and D (see pages 144-145). The 247 diamonds are set out in 17 alternating rows of 14 or 15 diamonds, with long and short half diamonds used as setting triangles around the edge of the quilt.

CUTTING OUT

Fabric is cut across the width unless otherwise stated.

Diamonds – Template A

Referring to the Cutting Diagram, cut 5in (12.7cm) strips across the width of the fabric (6 Template A diamonds can be cut from each strip, using either Cutting Diagram Method 1 or Method 2). Using the different cutting methods means each bias-cut edge is sewn to a grain-line edge, thereby strengthening the quilt and preventing it from stretching. Cut the first row of Template A diamonds using Method 1, the second row of diamonds using Method 2, and so on.
Note: If using a 60° ruler, use the manufacturer's instructions for cutting diamonds.

Fabric 2 (3 strips) 15 diamonds;
Fabric 3 (3 strips) 15 diamonds;
Fabric 4 (5 strips) 29 diamonds;
Fabric 5 (5 strips) 28 diamonds;
Fabric 6 (5 strips) 30 diamonds;
Fabric 7 (5 strips) 29 diamonds;
Fabric 8 (5 strips) 30 diamonds;
Fabric 9 (3 strips) 14 diamonds;
Fabric 10 (3 strips) 15 diamonds;
Fabric 11 (3 strips) 14 diamonds;
Fabric 12 (3 strips) 14 diamonds;
Fabric 13 (3 strips) 14 diamonds.

Setting Short Half and Quarter Diamonds – Templates B, C & C Reverse

From Fabric 1 cut 3 strips 5in (12.7cm) wide and cross cut 28 triangles using Template B, placing it on the grain line and rotating the ruler/template 180° after each cut. Each strip will yield 11 triangles. From the remaining piece cut 2 quarter diamonds using Template C and 2 using Template C Reverse, for the 4 corners of the quilt.

Setting Long Half Diamonds – Template D

From the remaining Fabric 1 cut 4 strips 3⅜in (8.6cm) wide. Using Template D, cut 16 long half diamonds, positioning the long side along the fabric edge and rotating the template 180° after each one. Each strip will yield 5 long half diamonds.

Backing

From Fabric 14 cut a piece 89in x 87in (226cm x 221cm).

Binding

From Fabric 15 cut 9 strips 2½in (6.4cm) wide. Remove selvedges and sew end to end with 45° seams (see page 149).

MAKING THE QUILT

Using a design wall will help to place patches in the required layout. Use ¼in (6mm) seams throughout.

Referring to the Quilt Assembly Diagram and quilt photograph for placement, arrange the diamond patches in rows. To vary the direction of the pattern and create a sense of movement, rotate some patches 180°. Add the side, top and bottom triangles and position the corner triangles.
Take care when handling the patches as they have some bias edges. A spritz of spray starch helps stabilize the raw edges.

Referring to the Quilt Assembly Diagram, sew the patches into diagonal rows, pressing the seams in opposite directions on alternate rows – odd rows to the left, even rows to the right – to allow the finished seams to sit flat.

Sew the diagonal rows together, taking care to match crossing seams, and press seams to complete the quilt top.

FINISHING THE QUILT

Press the quilt top and backing. Layer the quilt top, batting and backing, and baste together (see page 148).
Quilt as desired.
Trim the quilt edges and attach the binding (see page 149).

QUILT ASSEMBLY DIAGRAM

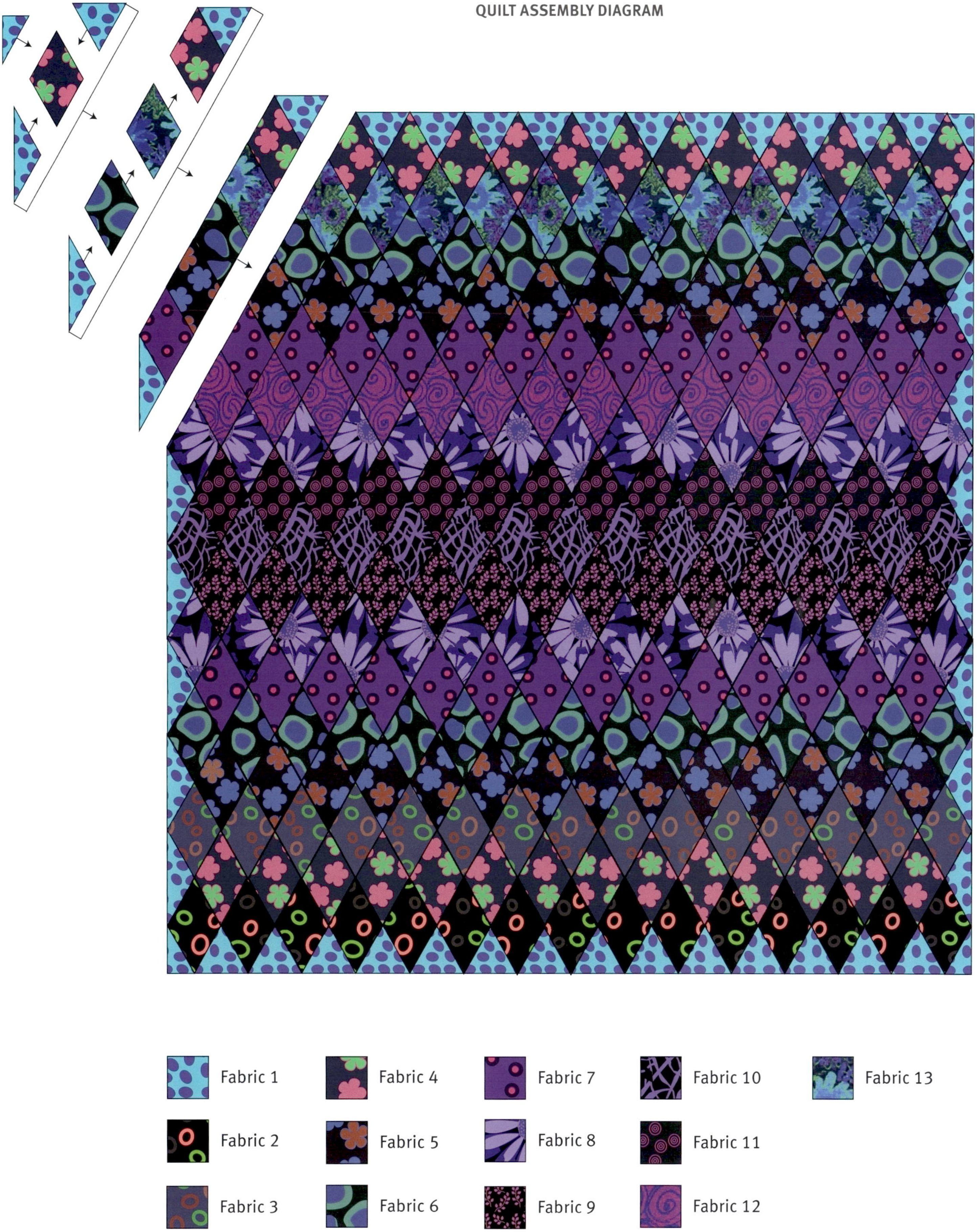

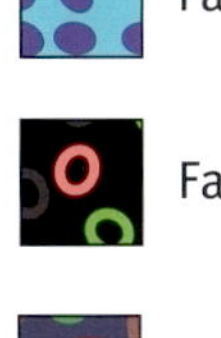
Fabric 1

Fabric 4

Fabric 7

Fabric 10

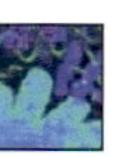
Fabric 13

Fabric 2

Fabric 5

Fabric 8

Fabric 11

Fabric 3

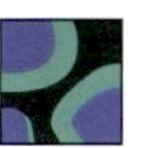
Fabric 6

Fabric 9

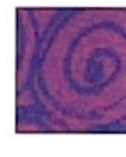
Fabric 12

contrast diamonds **

Kaffe Fassett

This selection of diamonds offers more contrasts both within each fabric choice as well as from row to row – creating an eclectic melding of prints. Follow the *Dark Diamonds* instructions on pages 69-71 but use the fabrics as listed here and shown in the Quilt Assembly Diagram.

SIZE OF FINISHED QUILT

81in x 79in (206cm x 201cm)

Patchwork Fabrics

PASHA PAISLEY		
Fabric 1	Black	7/8yd (85cm)
AMMONITES		
Fabric 2	Blue	3/4yd (70cm)
JUMBLE		
Fabric 3	Duck Egg	1/2yd (50cm)
Fabric 4	Rose	1/2yyd (50cm)
JAPONICA		
Fabric 5	Contrast	3/4yd (70cm)
BRASSICA		
Fabric 6	White	3/4yd (70cm)
BLOOMERS		
Fabric 7	Grey	3/4yd (70cm)
CACTUS FLOWER		
Fabric 8	Contrast	3/4yd (70cm)
Fabric 9	Black	1/2yyd (50cm)
PETALS		
Fabric 10	Black	1/2yyd (50cm)
SNOW FLOWER		
Fabric 11	Black	3/4yd (70cm)
BIG BLOOMS		
Fabric 12	Black	1/2yyd (50cm)

FABRIC SWATCH DIAGRAM

Patchwork Fabrics

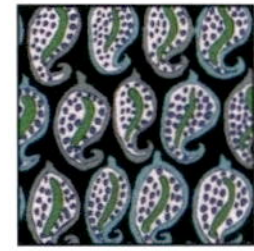

Fabric 1
PASHA PAISLEY
Black
BM96BK

Fabric 2
AMMONITES
Blue
PJ128BL

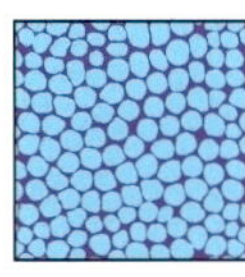

Fabric 3
JUMBLE
Duck Egg
BM53DE

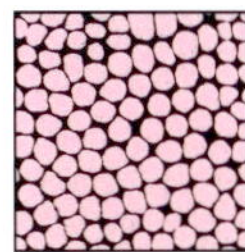

Fabric 4
JUMBLE
Rose
BM53RO

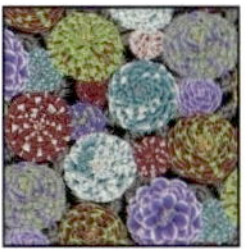

Fabric 5
JAPONICA
Contrast
PJ130CN

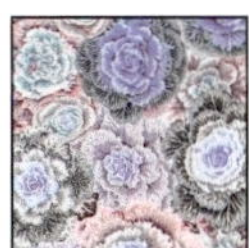

Fabric 6
BRASSICA
White
PJ51WH

Fabric 7
BLOOMERS
Grey
BM93GY

Fabric 8
CACTUS FLOWER
Contrast
PJ96CN

Fabric 9
CACTUS FLOWER
Black
PJ96BK

Fabric 10
PETALS
Black
GP201BK

Fabric 11
SNOW FLOWER
Black
BM94BK

Fabric 12
BIG BLOOMS
Black
GP91BK

INSTRUCTIONS

Contrast Diamonds is the same size as *Dark Diamonds* and is made in the same way, with a few minor alterations in the fabric requirements. Follow the cutting and making instructions for *Dark Diamonds* on pages 69-71 but replace the same-titled sections with the corresponding sections below.

Diamonds - Template A

Fabric 2 (5 strips) 30 diamonds;
Fabric 3 (3 strips) 14 diamonds;
Fabric 4 (3 strips) 15 diamonds;
Fabric 5 (5 strips) 30 diamonds;
Fabric 6 (5 strips) 28 diamonds;
Fabric 7 (5 strips) 29 diamonds;
Fabric 8 (5 strips) 29 diamonds;
Fabric 9 (3 strips) 14 diamonds;
Fabric 10 (3 strips) 15 diamonds;
Fabric 11 (5 strips) 28 diamonds;
Fabric 12 (3 strips) 15 diamonds.

FINISHING THE QUILT

This patchwork has been finished as a patchwork top. To prevent fraying, sew a double hem around the outer edge of the border to complete the top.

If you prefer to quilt your patchwork, cut batting and backing 8in (20.3cm) larger than the quilt top. Layer the quilt top, batting and backing, and baste together (see page 148).

Quilt as desired.

Trim the quilt edges and attach the binding (see page 149).

QUILT ASSEMBLY DIAGRAM

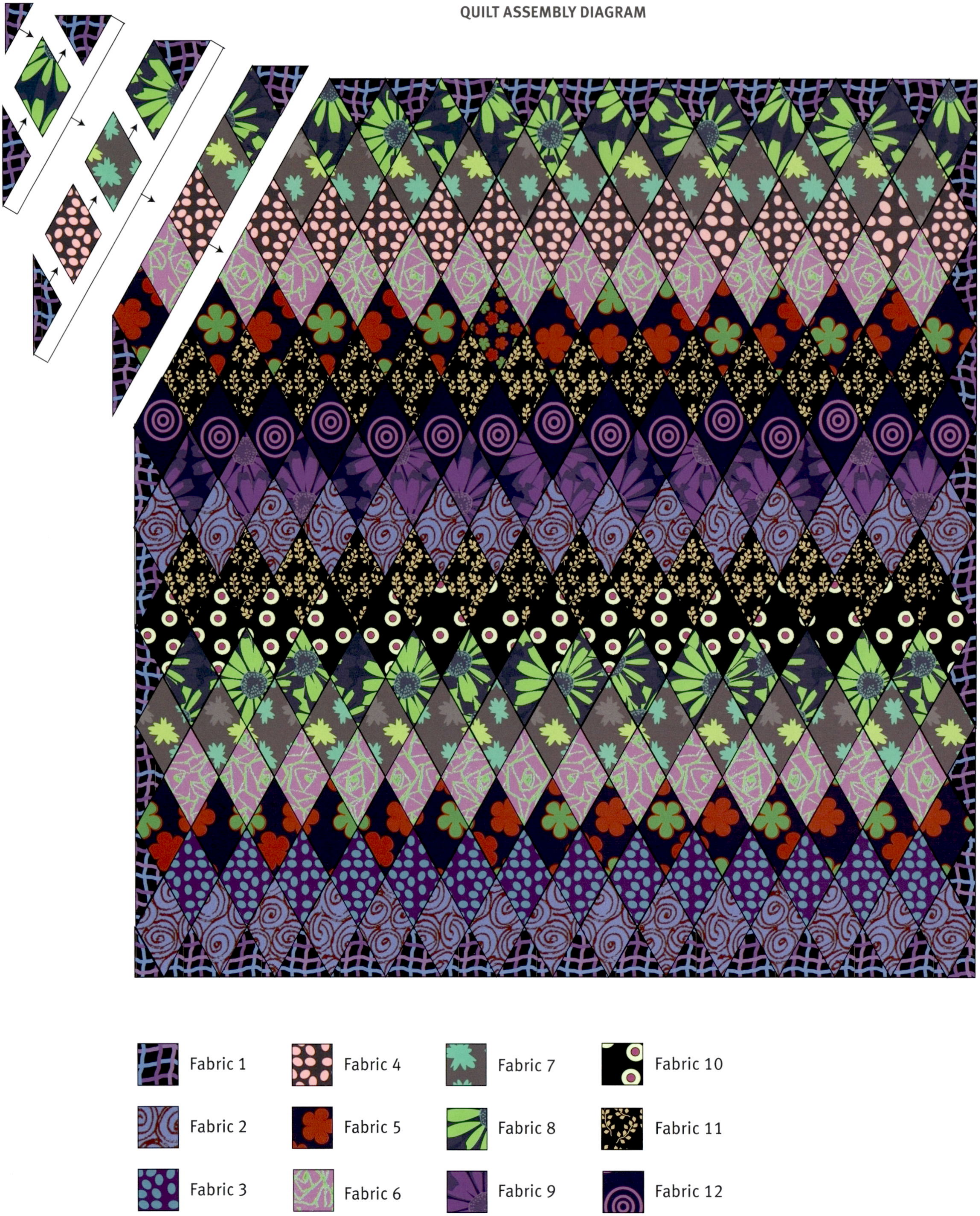

 Fabric 1

 Fabric 4

 Fabric 7

 Fabric 10

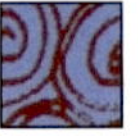 Fabric 2

 Fabric 5

 Fabric 8

 Fabric 11

 Fabric 3

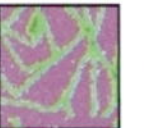 Fabric 6

 Fabric 9

 Fabric 12

hot diamonds **

Kaffe Fassett

The orange and red diamonds in this quilt blend beautifully, appearing to undulate from lighter to darker tones as well as from lighter to darker colours. Follow the *Dark Diamonds* instructions on pages 69-71 but use the fabrics as listed here and shown in the Quilt Assembly Diagram.

SIZE OF FINISHED QUILT

81in x 79in (206cm x 201cm)

Patchwork Fabrics

SPOT

Fabric 1	Orange	⅞yd (85cm)

BLOOMERS

Fabric 2	Green	¾yd (70cm)
Fabric 3	Orange	½yd (50cm)

CACTUS FLOWER

Fabric 4	Brown	½yd (50cm)

JAPANESE CHRYSANTHEMUM

Fabric 5	Brown	½yd (50cm)

URCHIN

Fabric 6	Red	¾yd (70cm)

FOLK FLOWER

Fabric 7	Red	¾yd (70cm)

FUNKY FLORA

Fabric 8	Forest	½yd (50cm)

PASHA PAISLEY

Fabric 9	Blue	½yd (50cm)
Fabric 10	Purple	½yd (50cm)

GAMEBOARD

Fabric 11	Red	½yd (50cm)

PAPAVER

Fabric 12	Red	¾yd (70cm)

WOBBLE

Fabric 13	Red	½yd (50cm)

BRASSICA

Fabric 14	Brown	½yd (50cm)

INSTRUCTIONS

Follow the cutting and making instructions for *Dark Diamonds* on pages 69-71 but replace the same-titled sections from it with the corresponding sections below.

Diamonds – Template A

Fabric 2 (5 strips) 29 diamonds;
Fabric 3 (3 strips) 14 diamonds;
Fabric 4 (3 strips) 14 diamonds;
Fabric 5 (3 strips) 15 diamonds;
Fabric 6 (5 strips) 29 diamonds;
Fabric 7 (5 strips) 30 diamonds;
Fabric 8 (3 strips) 14 diamonds;
Fabric 9 (3 strips) 15 diamonds;
Fabric 10 (3 strips) 14 diamonds;
Fabric 11 (3 strips) 15 diamonds;
Fabric 12 (5 strips) 28 diamonds;
Fabric 13 (3 strips) 15 diamonds;
Fabric 14 (3 strips) 15 diamonds.

FINISHING THE QUILT

This patchwork has been finished as a patchwork top. To prevent fraying, sew a double hem around the outer edge of the border to complete the top.

If you prefer to quilt your patchwork, cut batting and backing 8in (20.3cm) larger than the quilt top. Layer the quilt top, batting and backing, and baste together (see page 148).

Quilt as desired.

Trim the quilt edges and attach the binding (see page 149).

FABRIC SWATCH DIAGRAM

Patchwork Fabrics

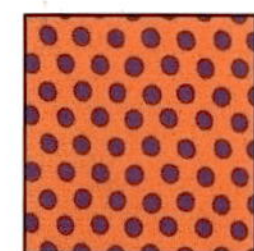

Fabric 1
SPOT
Orange
GP70OR

Fabric 2
BLOOMERS
Green
BM93GN

Fabric 3
BLOOMERS
Orange
BM93OR

Fabric 4
CACTUS FLOWER
Brown
PJ96BR

Fabric 5
JAPANESE CHRYSANTHEMUM
Brown
PJ41BR

Fabric 6
URCHIN
Red
PJ125RD

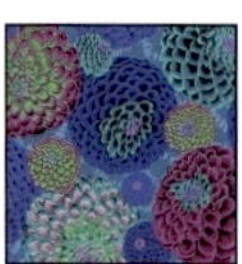

Fabric 7
FOLK FLOWER
Red
GP204RD

Fabric 8
FUNKY FLORA
Forest
BM11FO

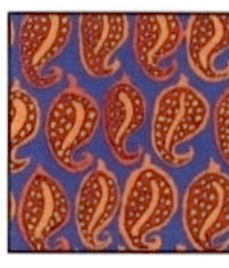

Fabric 9
PASHA PAISLEY
Blue
BM96BL

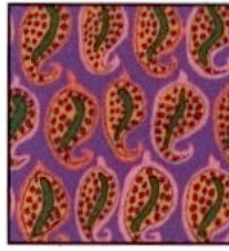

Fabric 10
PASHA PAISLEY
Purple
BM96PU

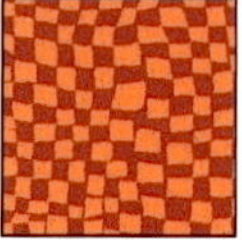

Fabric 11
GAMEBOARD
Red
BM95RD

Fabric 12
PAPAVER
Red
PJ127RD

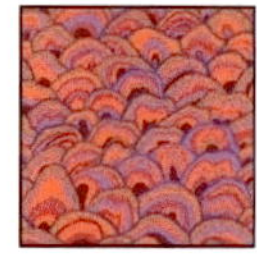

Fabric 13
WOBBLE
Red
BM92RD

Fabric 14
BRASSICA
Brown
PJ51BR

QUILT ASSEMBLY DIAGRAM

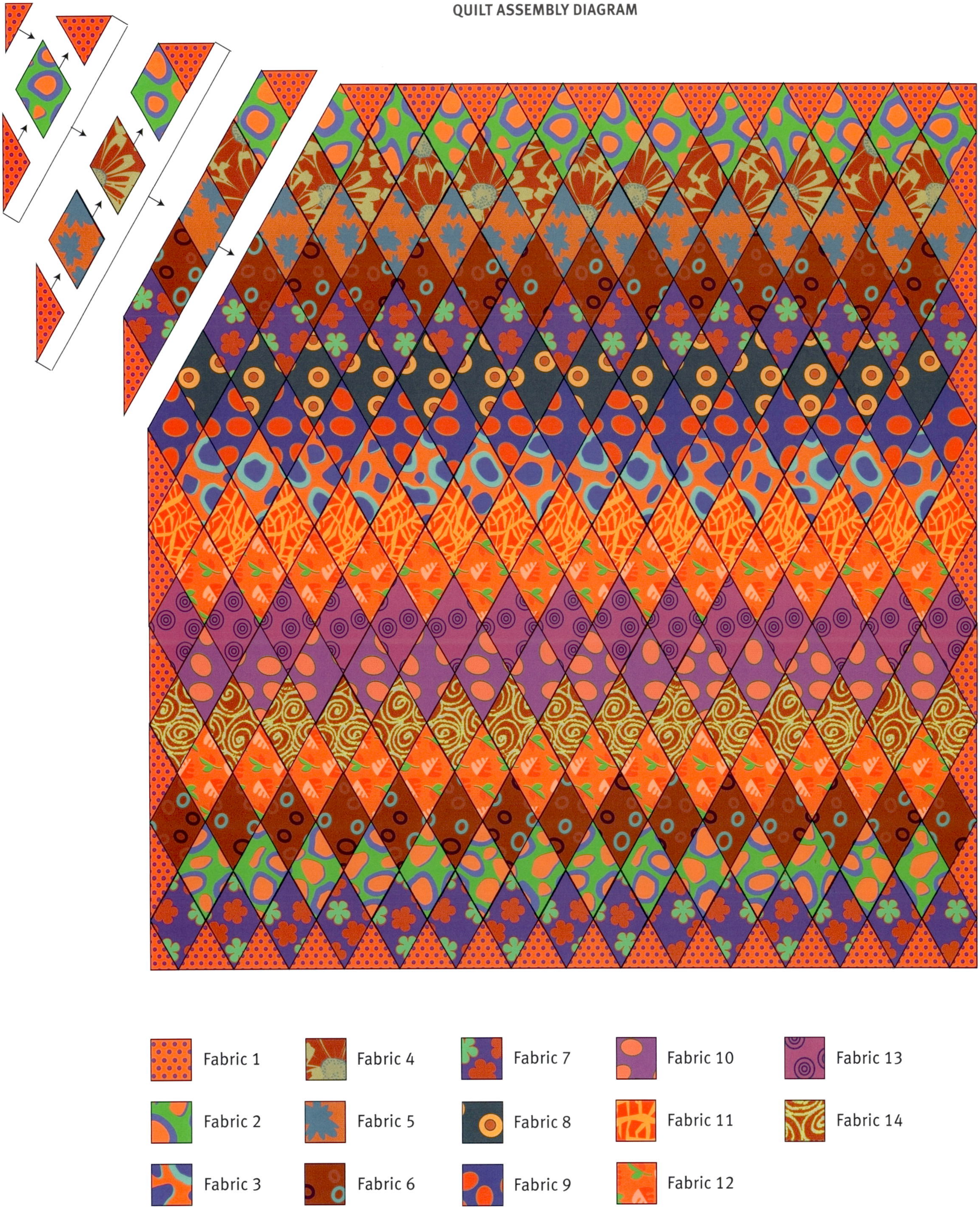

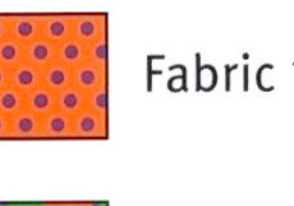
Fabric 1

Fabric 4

Fabric 7

Fabric 10

Fabric 13

Fabric 2

Fabric 5

Fabric 8

Fabric 11

Fabric 14

Fabric 3

Fabric 6

Fabric 9

Fabric 12

contrast roman tiles *

Kaffe Fassett

This format of split nine-square blocks with a border of half-square triangles is a fantastic way to play with contrast, whether in plain dark and light fabrics, in contrasting coloured prints or even in contrasting scales of prints.

Two further versions are included, each showcasing a different colour palette. The instructions for the alternatives follow the main quilt in terms of construction method but include their own fabric choices. For the backing and bindings of the alternatives, follow the main quilt instructions but choose your own backings and bindings from the lists on page 151.

SIZE OF FINISHED QUILT

64in x 64in (163cm x 163cm)

FABRICS

Fabrics have been calculated at a maximum width of 40in (102cm) and cut across the width, unless otherwise stated. Fabrics have been given a number – see Fabric Swatch Diagram for details.

Patchwork Fabrics

SPOT
Fabric 1 Pond ⅜yd (40cm)
* see also Binding Fabric
Fabric 2 Shocking ⅜yd (40cm)
MILLEFIORE
Fabric 3 Mauve 1⅜yd (1.3m)
BLOOMERS
Fabric 4 Cobalt ¼yd (25cm)
AMMONITES
Fabric 5 Pink ¼yd (25cm)
JAPONICA
Fabric 6 Blue ¼yd (25cm)
REFLECTIONS
Fabric 7 Lavender ¼yd (25cm)
Fabric 8 Sky ¼yd (25cm)
DREAM
Fabric 9 Blue ¼yd (25cm)
JUMBLE
Fabric 10 Yellow ¼yd (25cm)
Fabric 11 Bubblegum ⅜yd (40cm)
WOBBLE
Fabric 12 Blue 1⅜yd (1.3m)
URCHIN
Fabric 13 Blue ¼yd (25cm)
PAPAVER
Fabric 14 Green ¼yd (25cm)

FABRIC SWATCH DIAGRAM

Patchwork Fabrics

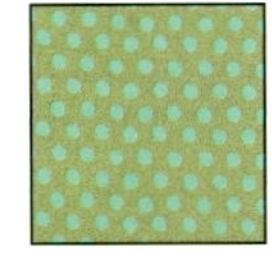

Fabric 1
SPOT
Pond
GP70PO

Fabric 2
SPOT
Shocking
GP70SG

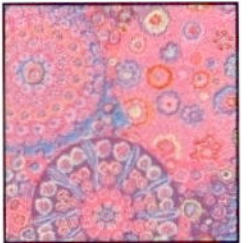

Fabric 3
MILLEFIORE
Mauve
GP92MV

Fabric 4
BLOOMERS
Cobalt
BM93CB

Fabric 5
AMMONITES
Pink
PJ128PK

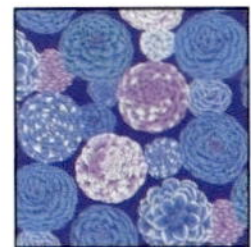

Fabric 6
JAPONICA
Blue
PJ130BL

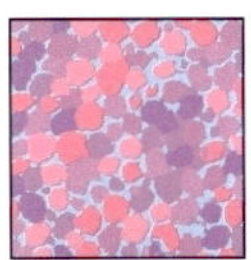

Fabric 7
REFLECTIONS
Lavender
BM87LV

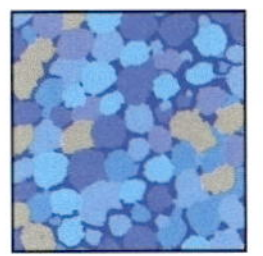

Fabric 8
REFLECTIONS
Sky
BM87SK

Fabric 9
DREAM
Blue
GP148BL

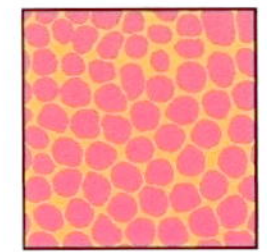

Fabric 10
JUMBLE
Yellow
BM53YE

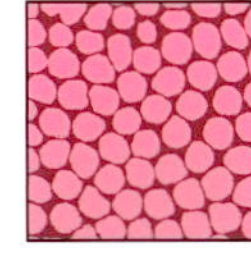

Fabric 11
JUMBLE
Bubblegum
BM53BB

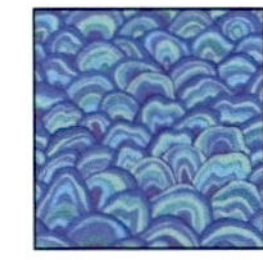

Fabric 12
WOBBLE
Blue
BM92BL

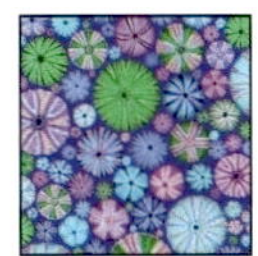

Fabric 13
URCHIN
Blue
PJ125BL

Fabric 14
PAPAVER
Green
PJ127GN

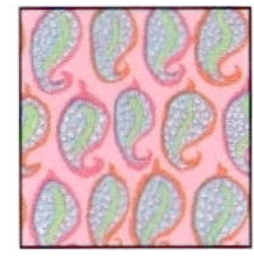

Fabric 15
PASHA PAISLEY
Pink
BM96PK

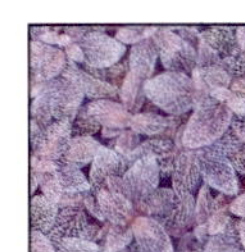

Fabric 16
FITTONIA
Blue
PJ129BL

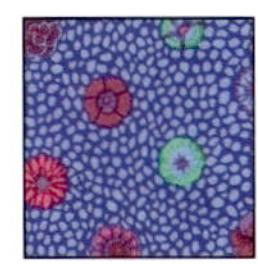

Fabric 17
GUINEA FLOWER
Cobalt
GP59CB

Backing and Binding Fabrics

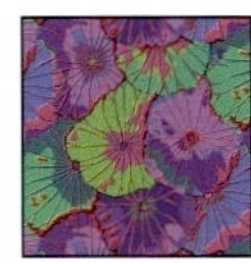

Fabric 18
LOTUS LEAF
Purple
QB07PU

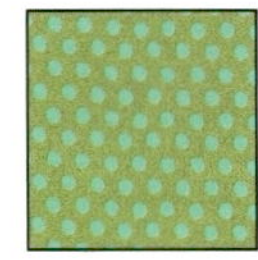

Fabric 1
SPOT
Pond
GP70PO

PASHA PAISLEY

Fabric 15	Pink	¼yd (25cm)

FITTONIA

Fabric 16	Blue	¼yd (25cm)

GUINEA FLOWER

Fabric 17	Cobalt	¼yd (25cm)

Backing and Binding Fabrics

LOTUS LEAF extra-wide backing

Fabric 18	Purple	2yd (1.9m)

SPOT

Fabric 1	Pond	⅝yd (60cm)

* see also Patchwork Fabrics

Batting

72in x 72in (183cm x 183cm)

PATCHES

The split nine-patch block is 12in (30.5cm) square finished and is made using square and half-square triangle (HST) patches, both forming finished 4in (10.2cm) squares. The blocks are straight set into rows with a border made of HST squares the same size.

CUTTING OUT

Fabric is cut across the width unless otherwise stated. When cutting different pieces from the same fabric, always cut the larger pieces first. In this quilt, cut the larger strips for the triangle patches first, then trim down any remaining strips to the smaller width required for the squares. For best results, use spray starch before cutting.

Triangle Patches

Cut strips 4⅞in (12.3cm) wide and cross cut squares at 4⅞in (12.3cm). Each strip will yield 8 squares. Cut each square diagonally once to form two HSTs. Cut a total of 288 HSTs from fabrics as follows.

Fabric 2 (1 strip) 3 squares – 6 triangles;
Fabric 3 (8 strips) 58 squares – 116 triangles;
Fabric 4 (1 strip) 2 squares – 4 triangles;
Fabric 5 (1 strip) 2 squares – 4 triangles;
Fabric 6 (1 strip) 2 squares – 4 triangles;
Fabric 7 (1 strip) 2 squares – 4 triangles;
Fabric 8 (1 strip) 2 squares – 4 triangles;
Fabric 9 (1 strip) 2 squares – 4 triangles;
Fabric 10 (1 strip) 2 squares – 4 triangles;
Fabric 11 (1 strip) 3 squares – 6 triangles;
Fabric 12 (8 strips) 58 squares – 116 triangles;
Fabric 13 (1 strip) 2 squares – 4 triangles;

BLOCK ASSEMBLY DIAGRAM

a

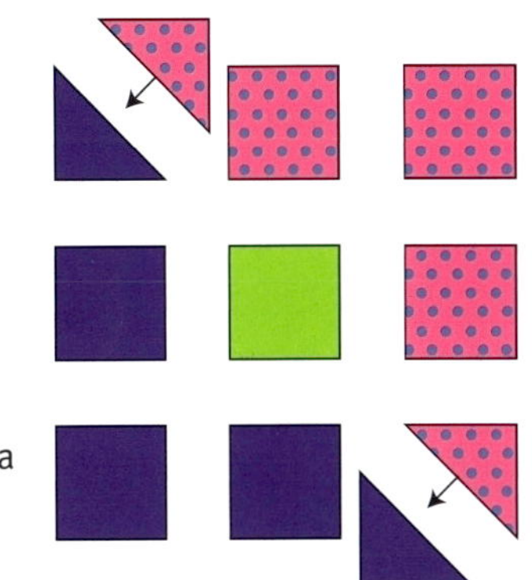

b

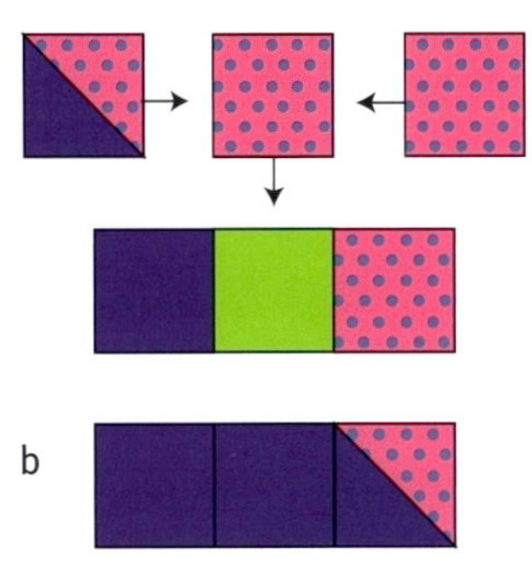

c

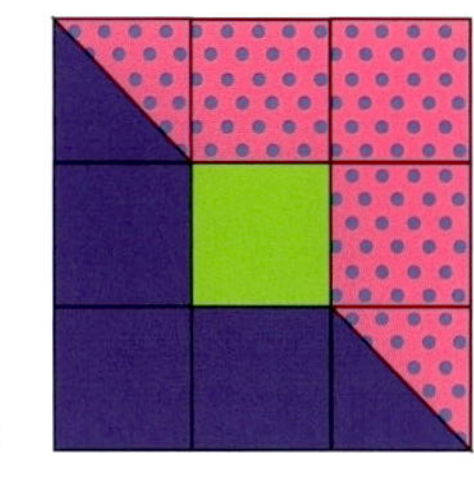

Fabric 14 (1 strip) 2 squares – 4 triangles;
Fabric 15 (1 strip) 2 squares – 4 triangles;
Fabric 16 (1 strip) 1 square – 2 triangles;
Fabric 17 (1 strip) 1 square – 2 triangles.

Square Patches
From the remaining Fabrics 1-17 trim any remaining strips from above (shown below as +) to 4½in (11.4cm) wide, then if necessary cut further strips 4½in (11.4cm) wide and cross cut 4½in (11.4cm) squares. Each strip will yield 8 squares. Cut a total of 112 squares from fabrics as follows:
Fabric 1 (2 strips) 16 squares;
Fabric 2 (1 strip +) 9 squares;
Fabric 3 (+ from remaining) 6 squares;
Fabric 4 (+ from remaining) 6 squares;
Fabric 5 (+ from remaining) 6 squares;
Fabric 6 (+ from remaining) 6 squares;
Fabric 7 (+ from remaining) 6 squares;
Fabric 8 (+ from remaining) 6 squares;
Fabric 9 (+ from remaining) 6 squares;
Fabric 10 (+ from remaining) 6 squares;
Fabric 11 (1 strip +) 9 squares;
Fabric 12 (+ from remaining) 6 squares;
Fabric 13 (+ from remaining) 6 squares;
Fabric 14 (+ f rom remaining) 6 squares;
Fabric 15 (+ from remaining) 6 squares;
Fabric 16 (+ from remaining) 3 squares;
Fabric 17 (+ from remaining) 3 squares.

Backing
From Fabric 18 cut a piece 72in x 72in (183cm x 183cm).

Binding
From Fabric 1 cut 7 strips 2½in (6.4cm) wide. Remove selvedges and sew end to end with 45° seams (see page 149).

MAKING THE QUILT
Using a design wall will help to place the patches in the required layout.
Use ¼in (6mm) seams throughout.

Split Nine-square Blocks
Referring to the Block Assembly Diagram, select 3 matching pink square patches and 2 HSTs, 3 matching blue square patches and 2 HSTs and a Fabric 1 centre square.
Sew the pink and blue triangles together along their long edge to make 2 HST squares (a) and press lightly. Arrange the pieced squares with the other patches to form the block (b) and sew together in rows of 3, then sew the 3 rows together, taking care to match crossing seams, to create the finished block (c). Make 16 blocks.

Assembling the Quilt
Referring to the Quilt Assembly Diagram and quilt photograph for placement, arrange the blocks with the pink halves positioned top right and the blue halves positioned lower left. Sew the blocks together into 4 rows of 4, pressing the seams in opposite directions on alternate rows – odd rows to the left, even rows to the right – to allow the finished seams to sit flat. Press seams and sew the 4 rows together, taking care to match crossing seams.

Borders
Sew pink and blue HSTs together along their longer edge, taking care not to stretch these bias seams. Lightly press all seams towards the blue triangles.

Lay out 4 rows of 12 HST squares for the top and bottom borders, ensuring the blue triangles are positioned top right and the pink triangles are positioned lower left – the **opposite** way from the centre blocks. Sew each row of HSTs together, then sew 2 rows together for the top border and 2 rows together for the bottom border.
Lay out 4 columns of 16 HST squares for the side borders, again ensuring the blue triangles are positioned top right and the pink triangles are positioned lower left – the **opposite** way from the centre blocks. Sew each column of HSTs together, then sew 2 columns together for each side border.

After a final check to make sure the HST squares are all positioned correctly, pin then sew a double row of 12 HSTs to the top and bottom of the centre and lightly press seams. Pin then sew a double column of HSTs to each side of the centre to complete the quilt top.

FINISHING THE QUILT
Press the quilt top. Layer the quilt top, batting and backing, and baste together (see page 148).
Quilt as desired.
Trim the quilt edges and attach the binding (see page 149).

QUILT ASSEMBLY DIAGRAM

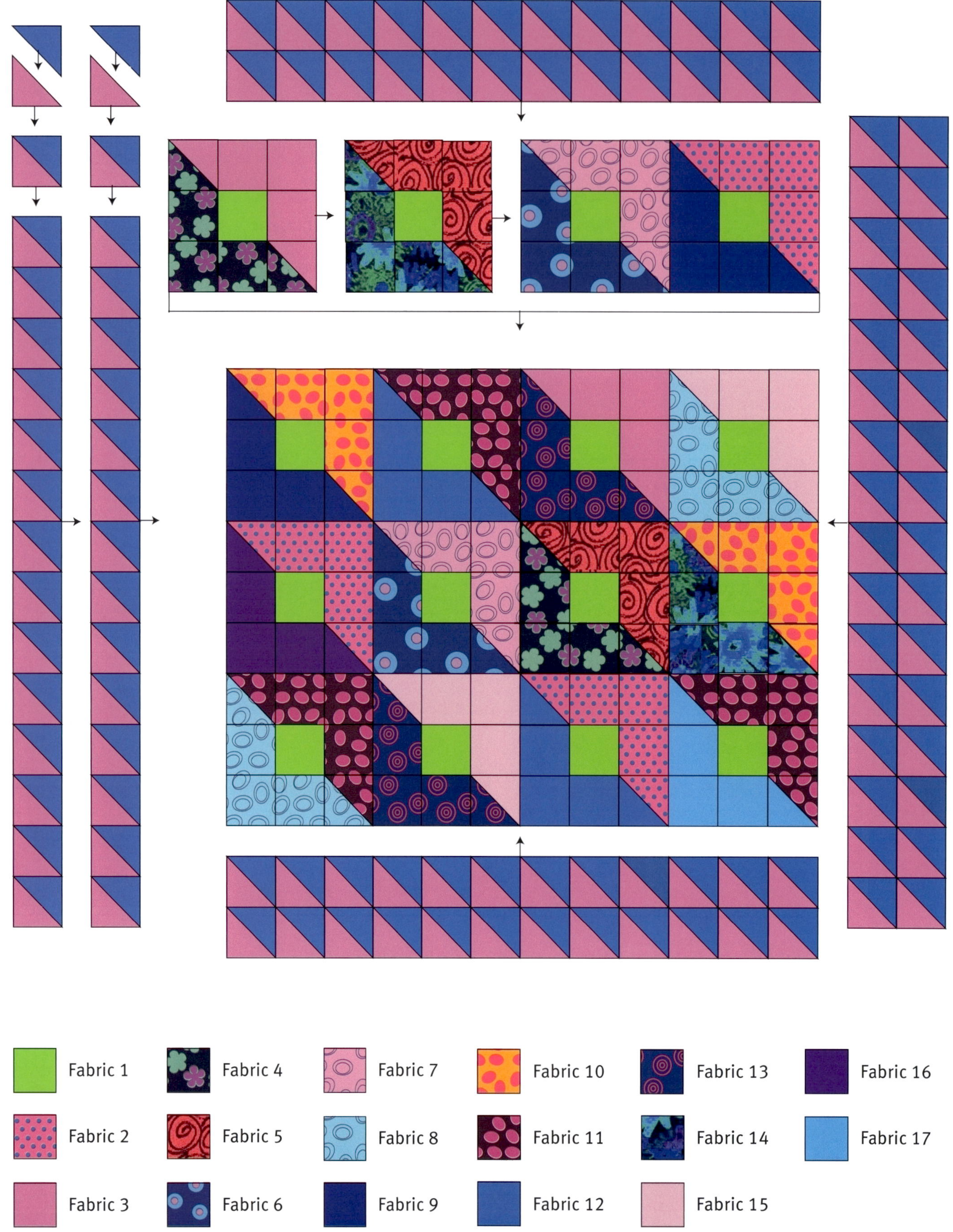

warm roman tiles **

Kaffe Fassett

This dark beauty is like shafts of sunset breaking through a forest canopy. A variation of the split nine-patch, it sports a large print border with fussy-cut cornerstones in place of the half-square triangles border.

Follow the *Contrast Roman Tiles* quilt instructions on pages 79-82 but use the fabrics as listed here and shown in the Quilt Assembly Diagram.

SIZE OF FINISHED QUILT

64in x 64in (163cm x 163cm)

FABRICS

Fabrics have been calculated at a maximum width of 40in (102cm) and cut across the width, unless otherwise stated. Fabrics have been given a number – see Fabric Swatch Diagram for details.

Patchwork Fabrics

BLOOMERS		
Fabric 1	Green	¼yd (25cm)
Fabric 2	Orange	¼yd (25cm)
Fabric 3	Black	¼yd (25cm)
AMMONITES		
Fabric 4	Dark	1⅜yd (1.3m)
FOLK FLOWER		
Fabric 5	Purple	¼yd (25cm)
Fabric 6	Dark	¼yd (25cm)
Fabric 7	Red	¼yd (25cm)
REFLECTIONS		
Fabric 8	Brown	¼yd (25cm)
BRASSICA		
Fabric 9	Rust	¼yd (25cm)
CLOISONNÉ		
Fabric 10	Purple	¼yd (25cm)
URCHIN		
Fabric 11	Red	¼yd (25cm)
PAPAVER		
Fabric 12	Orange	¼yd (25cm)
Fabric 13	Red	¼yd (25cm)
PASHA PAISLEY		
Fabric 14	Blue	¼yd (25cm)
FITTONIA		
Fabric 15	Green	¼yd (25cm)
JAPONICA		
Fabric 16	Dark	½yd (50cm)
SHOT COTTON		
Fabric 17	Pimento	¼yd (25cm)
Fabric 18	Bloom	¼yd (25cm)
Fabric 19	Teal	¼yd (25cm)
Fabric 20	Pine	¼yd (25cm)
Fabric 21	Aubergine	¼yd (25cm)

FABRIC SWATCH DIAGRAM

Patchwork Fabrics

Fabric 1
BLOOMERS
Green
BM93GN

Fabric 2
BLOOMERS
Orange
BM93OR

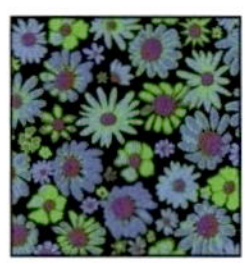

Fabric 3
BLOOMERS
Black
BM93BK

Fabric 4
AMMONITES
Dark
PJ128DK

Fabric 5
FOLK FLOWER
Purple
GP204PU

Fabric 6
FOLK FLOWER
Dark
GP204DK

Fabric 7
FOLK FLOWER
Red
GP204RD

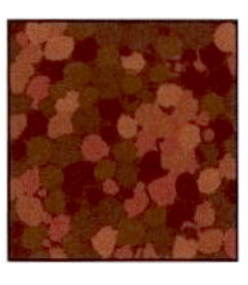

Fabric 8
REFLECTIONS
Brown
BM087BR

Fabric 9
BRASSICA
Rust
PJ051RU

Fabric 10
CLOISONNÉ
Purple
GP46PU

Fabric 11
URCHIN
Red
PJ125RD

Fabric 12
PAPAVER
Orange
PJ127OR

Fabric 13
PAPAVER
Red
PJ127RD

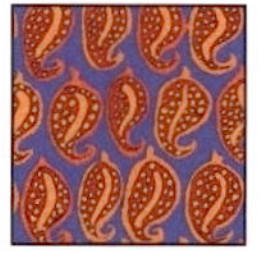

Fabric 14
PASHA PAISLEY
Blue
BM96BL

Fabric 15
FITTONIA
Green
PJ129GN

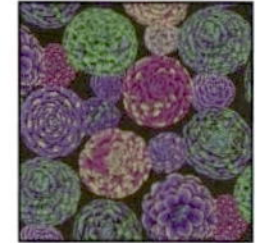

Fabric 16
JAPONICA
Dark
PJ130DK

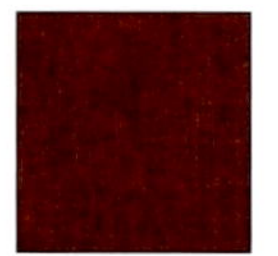

Fabric 17
SHOT COTTON
Pimento
SC116PI

Fabric 18
SHOT COTTON
Bloom
SC126BM

Fabric 19
SHOT COTTON
Teal
SC105TE

Fabric 20
SHOT COTTON
Pine
SC120PY

Fabric 21
SHOT COTTON
Aubergine
SC117AB

INSTRUCTIONS

Follow the cutting and making instructions for *Contrast Roman Tiles* on pages 79-82 but replace the same-titled sections from it with the corresponding sections below.

Border and Corner Squares

From **Fabric 4** cut 5 strips 8½in (21.6cm) wide. Join strips end to end to obtain the required length, using ¼in (6mm) seams, and press seams open. From the length cut 4 border pieces 48½in x 8½in (123.2cm x 21.6cm).
From **Fabric 16** fussy cut 4 squares at 8½in (21.6cm) with a flower centred approximately in the square.

Triangle Patches

Cut a strip 4⅞in (12.3cm) wide and cross cut 2 squares at 4⅞in (12.3cm) from each of **Fabrics 1-16**. Cut each square diagonally once to form two HSTs, 4 from each fabric giving a total of 64 HSTs.

Square Patches

From the remaining **Fabrics 1-16** trim each strip to 4½in (11.4cm) wide and cross cut 6 squares at 4½in (11.4cm) from each strip, to make a total of 96 squares.

Centre Squares

Cut a strip 4½in (11.4cm) wide and cross cut squares at 4½in (11.4cm) to make 16 squares in total from fabrics as follows:
Fabric 17 4 squares;
Fabric 18 3 squares;
Fabric 19 2 squares;
Fabric 20 4 squares;
Fabric 21 3 squares.

Split Nine-square Blocks

Referring to the Block Assembly Diagram on page 81, select 3 matching red square patches and 2 HSTs, 3 matching green square patches and 2 HSTs and a centre square. Sew the red and green triangles together along their long edge to make 2 HST squares and follow the instructions for making the blocks on page 81.

Referring to the Quilt Assembly Diagram and quilt photograph for placement, arrange the blocks with the red halves positioned top right and the green halves positioned lower left and follow instructions for assembling the quilt on page 81.

Border

Pin and sew a **Fabric 4** border piece to each side of the centre and press seams towards the border.
Sew a **Fabric 16** corner square to each end of the remaining border pieces and press seams towards the border.
Pin and sew the 2 remaining border/corner sections to the top and bottom of the quilt, taking care to match crossing seams.

FINISHING THE QUILT

This patchwork has been finished as a patchwork top. To prevent fraying, sew a double hem around the outer edge of the border to complete the top.
If you prefer to quilt your patchwork, cut batting and backing 8in (20.3cm) larger than the quilt top. Layer the quilt top, batting and backing, and baste together (see page 148).
Quilt as desired.
Trim the quilt edges and attach the binding (see page 149).

QUILT ASSEMBLY DIAGRAM

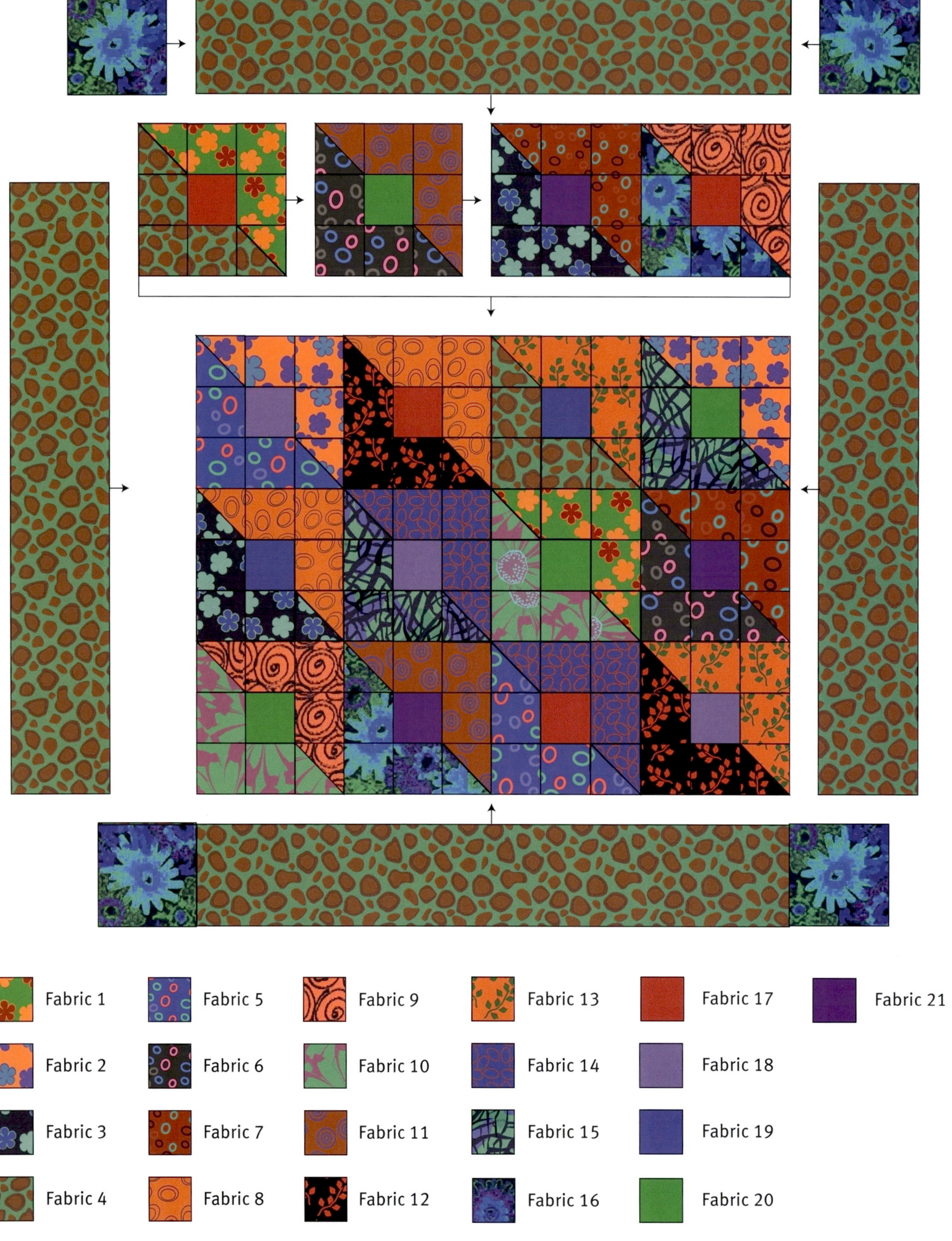

dark roman tiles *

Kaffe Fassett

This dark split nine-square quilt has some pops of exciting colour in its block centres and a beautiful cool leafy surround with Philip Jacobs' Jungle print border.

Follow the *Contrast Roman Tiles* quilt instructions on pages 79-82 but use the fabrics as listed here and shown in the Quilt Assembly Diagram.

SIZE OF FINISHED QUILT

66in x 66in (168cm x 168cm)

FABRICS

Fabrics have been calculated at a maximum width of 40in (102cm) and cut across the width, unless otherwise stated. Fabrics have been given a number – see Fabric Swatch Diagram for details.

Patchwork Fabrics

LOTUS LEAF		
Fabric 1	Grey	⅜yd (40cm)
Fabric 2	Dark	¼yd (25cm)
BRASSICA		
Fabric 3	Grey	¼yd (25cm)
AMMONITES		
Fabric 4	Blue	¼yd (25cm)
Fabric 5	Dark	¼yd (25cm)
ASIAN CIRCLES		
Fabric 6	Turquoise	¼yd (25cm)
PASHA PAISLEY		
Fabric 7	Black	¼yd (25cm)
JAPONICA		
Fabric 8	Pastel	¼yd (25cm)
PAPAVER		
Fabric 9	Grey	¼yd (25cm)
JUMBLE		
Fabric 10	Grey	¼yd (25cm)
SAILOR VALENTINE		
Fabric 11	Grey	¼yd (25cm)
FITTONIA		
Fabric 12	Blue	¼yd (25cm)
REFLECTIONS		
Fabric 13	Moss	¼yd (25cm)
Fabric 14	Putty	¼yd (25cm)
JUNGLE		
Fabric 15	Lavender	⅜yd (40cm)
Fabric 16	Neutral	1⅜yd (1.3m)
GAMEBOARD		
Fabric 17	Purple	¼yd (25cm)
Fabric 18	Red	¼yd (25cm)
Fabric 19	Pink	¼yd (25cm)
SPOT		
Fabric 20	Shocking	¼yd (25cm)
ABORIGINAL DOT		
Fabric 21	Cantaloupe	¼yd (25cm)
SHOT COTTON		
Fabric 22	Paprika	¼yd (25cm)
Fabric 23	Glacier	¼yd (25cm)
Fabric 24	Camelia	¼yd (25cm)

INSTRUCTIONS

Follow the cutting and making instructions for *Contrast Roman Tiles* on pages 79-82 but replace the same-titled sections from it with the corresponding sections below.

Border

From **Fabric 16** cut 5 strips 9½in (24.1cm) wide. Join strips end to end using ¼in (6mm) seams, and press seams open.
From the length cut:
2 border pieces 48½in x 9½in (123.2cm x 24.1cm) for the top and bottom borders;
2 border pieces 66½in x 9½in (168.9cm x 24.1cm) for the side borders.

Triangle Patches

Cut a strip 4⅞in (12.3cm) wide and cross cut squares at 4⅞in (12.3cm). Cut each square diagonally once to form two HSTs, making a total of 64 HSTs from fabrics as follows:
From **Fabric 1 and 15** cut 3 squares – 6 triangles;
From **Fabrics 2-14** cut 2 squares – 4 triangles.

Square Patches

Trim the remaining **Fabrics 1 and 15** to 4½in (11.4cm) wide and cut a second strip 4½in (11.4cm) wide. Cross cut 9 squares at 4½in (11.4cm) in each fabric.
From the remaining **Fabrics 2-14** trim the strip to 4½in (11.4cm) wide and cross cut 6 squares at 4½in (11.4cm) from each strip, to make a total of 96 squares.

Centre Squares

Cut a strip 4½in (11.4cm) wide and cross cut squares at 4½in (11.4cm) to make 16 squares in total from fabrics as follows:
Fabric 17 (1 strip) 2 squares;
Fabric 18 (1 strip) 3 squares;
Fabric 19 (1 strip) 1 square;
Fabric 20 (1 strip) 2 squares;
Fabric 21 (1 strip) 2 squares;
Fabric 22 (1 strip) 2 squares;
Fabric 23 (1 strip) 2 squares;
Fabric 24 (1 strip) 2 squares.

Split Nine-square Blocks

Referring to the Block Assembly Diagram on page 81, select 3 matching pale square patches and 2 HSTs, 3 matching dark square patches and 2 HSTs and a centre square. Sew the pale and dark triangles together along their long edge to make 2 HST squares and follow the instructions for making the blocks on page 81.

Referring to the Quilt Assembly Diagram and photograph for placement, arrange the blocks with the pale halves positioned top right and the dark halves positioned lower left and follow instructions for assembling the quilt on page 81.

Border

Pin and sew a **Fabric 16** border piece to the top and bottom of the quilt centre and press seams towards the border. Pin and sew the 2 remaining border pieces to each side of the quilt to complete the quilt top.

FINISHING THE QUILT

This patchwork has been finished as a patchwork top. To prevent fraying, sew a double hem around the outer edge of the border to complete the top.
If you prefer to quilt your patchwork, cut batting and backing 8in (20.3cm) larger than the quilt top. Layer the quilt top, batting and backing, and baste together (see page 148).
Quilt as desired.
Trim the quilt edges and attach the binding (see page 149).

FABRIC SWATCH DIAGRAM

Patchwork Fabrics

Fabric 1
LOTUS LEAF
Grey
GP29GY

Fabric 2
LOTUS LEAF
Dark
GP29DK

Fabric 3
BRASSICA
Grey
PJ51GY

Fabric 4
AMMONITES
Blue
PJ128BL

Fabric 5
AMMONITES
Dark
PJ128DK

Fabric 6
ASIAN CIRCLES
Turquoise
GP89TQ

Fabric 7
PASHA PAISLEY
Black
BM96BK

Fabric 8
JAPONICA
Pastel
PJ130PT

Fabric 9
PAPAVER
Grey
PJ127GY

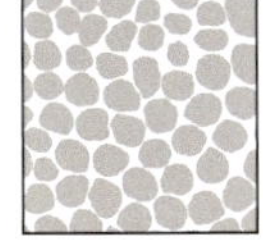

Fabric 10
JUMBLE
Grey
BM53GY

Fabric 11
SAILOR VALENTINE
Grey
PJ121GY

Fabric 12
FITTONIA
Blue
PJ129BL

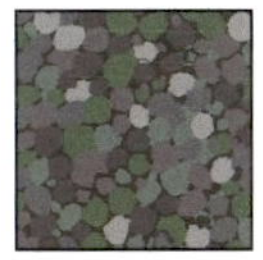

Fabric 13
REFLECTIONS
Moss
BM87MS

Fabric 14
REFLECTIONS
Putty
BM87PT

Fabric 15
JUNGLE
Lavender
PJ126LV

Fabric 16
JUNGLE
Neutral
PJ126NE

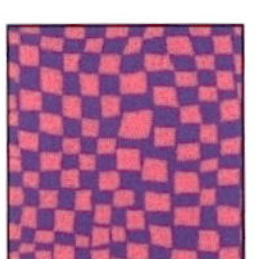

Fabric 17
GAMEBOARD
Purple
BM95PU

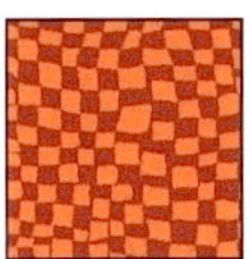

Fabric 18
GAMEBOARD
Red
BM95RD

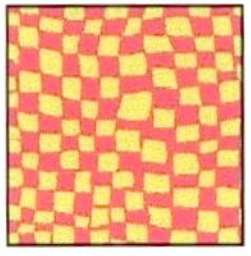

Fabric 19
GAMEBOARD
Pink
PWBM095

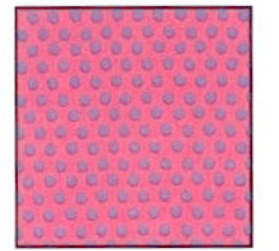

Fabric 20
SPOT
Shocking
GP70SG

Fabric 21
ABORIGINAL DOT
Cantaloupe
GP71CA

Fabric 22
SHOT COTTON
Paprika
SC101PP

Fabric 23
SHOT COTTON
Glacier
SC124GL

Fabric 24
SHOT COTTON
Camelia
SC109CX

QUILT ASSEMBLY DIAGRAM

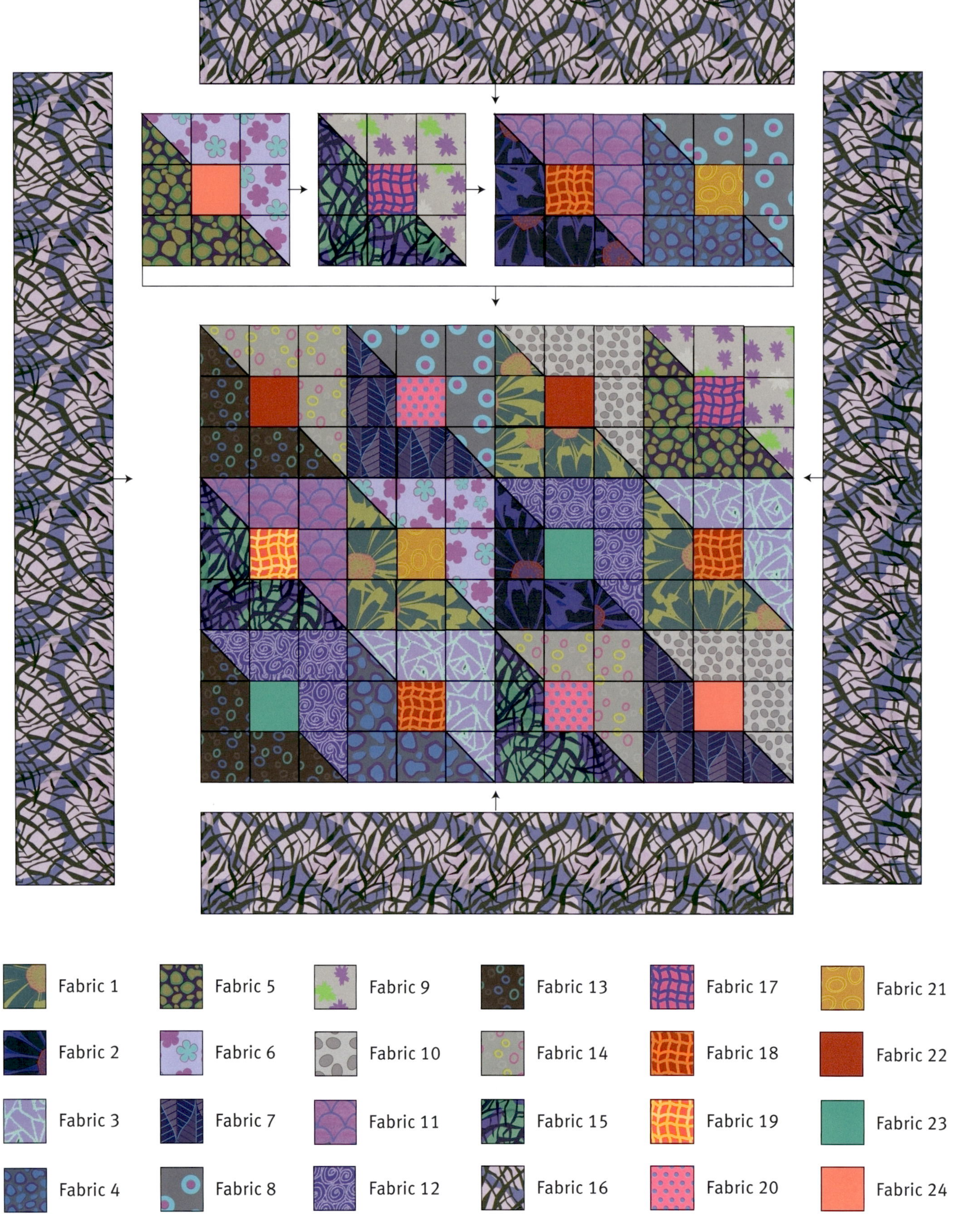

moody snowball criss cross **

Liza Prior Lucy

This is the first of three snowball block variations, namely crosses, circles and stars. Two further snowball quilts follow, each showcasing different colour palettes, and each highlighting alternative snowball constructions. At first glance the crosses in this quilt are more prominent than the snowballs. Liza has contrasted the crosses beautifully with my cool blue colourway of Philip's Ammonites print.

SIZE OF FINISHED QUILT
80in x 80in (203cm x 203cm)

FABRICS
Fabrics have been calculated at a maximum width of 40in (102cm). Fabrics have been given a number – see the Fabric Swatch Diagram for details.

Patchwork Fabrics

AMMONITES		
Fabric 1	Blue	2¾yd (2.6m)
SPOT		
Fabric 2	Black	1yd (95cm)
Fabric 3	Storm	⅜yd (40cm)
Fabric 4	Steel	¼yd (25cm)
ABORIGINAL DOT		
Fabric 5	Turquoise	1yd (95cm)
* see also Binding Fabric		
Fabric 6	Iris	⅜yd (40cm)
Fabric 7	Periwinkle	⅜yd (40cm)
ROMAN GLASS		
Fabric 8	Blue and White	⅜yd (40cm)
Fabric 9	Grey	¼yd (25cm)
PAPERWEIGHT		
Fabric 10	Sludge	¼yd (25cm)
GUINEA FLOWER		
Fabric 11	Cobalt	⅜yd (40cm)
Fabric 12	Grey	¼yd (25cm)
MILLEFIORE		
Fabric 13	Grey	¼yd (25cm)
PALM LEAVES		
Fabric 14	Contrast	2¼yd (2.1m)

Backing and Binding Fabrics

ONION RINGS extra-wide backing		
Fabric 15	Black	2½yd (2.3m)
ABORIGINAL DOT		
Fabric 5	Turquoise	¾yd (70cm)
* see also Patchwork Fabrics		

Batting
88in x 88in (224cm x 224cm)

FABRIC SWATCH DIAGRAM

Patchwork Fabrics

Fabric 1
AMMONITES
Blue
PJ128BL

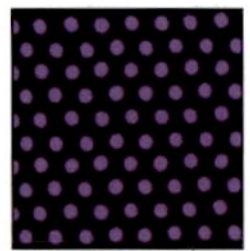
Fabric 2
SPOT
Black
GP70BK

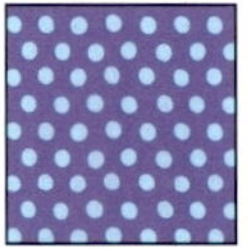
Fabric 3
SPOT
Storm
GP70SR

Fabric 4
SPOT
Steel
GP70ST

Fabric 5
ABORIGINAL DOT
Turquoise
GP71TQ

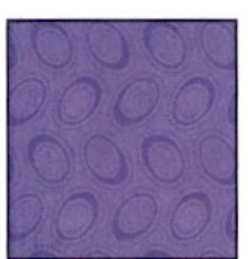
Fabric 6
ABORIGINAL DOT
Iris
GP71IR

Fabric 7
ABORIGINAL DOT
Periwinkle
GP71PE

Fabric 8
ROMAN GLASS
Blue and White
GP01BW

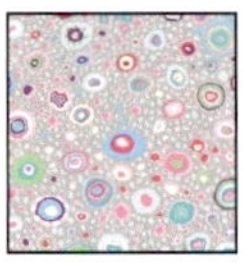
Fabric 9
ROMAN GLASS
Grey
GP01GY

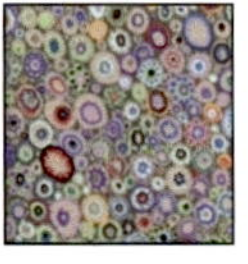
Fabric 10
PAPERWEIGHT
Sludge
GP20SL

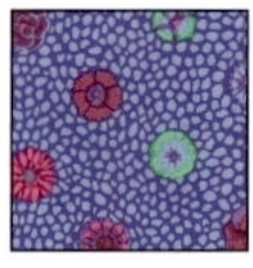
Fabric 11
GUINEA FLOWER
Cobalt
GP59CB

Fabric 12
GUINEA FLOWER
Grey
GP59GY

Fabric 13
MILLEFIORE
Grey
GP92GY

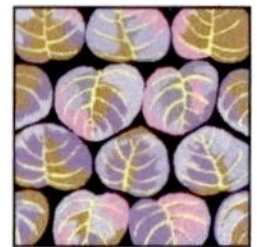
Fabric 14
PALM LEAVES
Contrast
GP208CN

Backing and Binding Fabrics

Fabric 15
ONION RINGS
Black
QM01BK

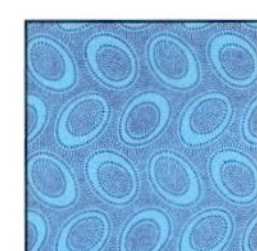
Fabric 5
ABORIGINAL DOT
Turquoise
GP71TQ

SNOWBALL BLOCK ASSEMBLY DIAGRAM

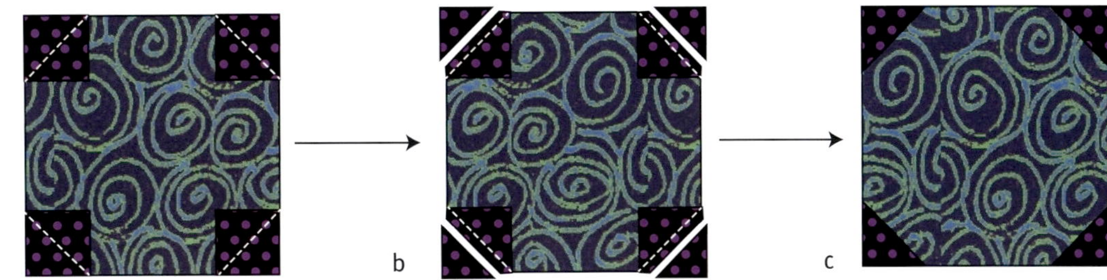

PATCHES

Each of the three quilt variations alternates a snowball block with a different feature block. The snowball blocks in all three quilts are the same size, 8in (20.3cm) finished squares, but use different fabrics.

The feature blocks in this quilt are 8in (20.3cm) finished X blocks. Patches are squares and half- and quarter-square triangles. A cross shape, made from 5 squares, is set on point with side-setting triangles (cut as quarter-square triangles) and corner-setting triangles (cut as half-square triangles). Alternating blocks are set in 9 rows of 9 blocks and surrounded with a 4in (10.2cm) finished border.

CUTTING OUT

Fabric is cut across the width unless otherwise stated. When cutting different pieces from the same fabric, always cut the larger pieces first.

Snowball Blocks

From **Fabric 1** cut 11 strips 8½in (21.6cm) wide and cross cut 41 squares at 8½in (21.6cm). Each strip yields 4 squares.

From **Fabric 2** cut 11 strips 2½in (6.4cm) wide and cross cut 164 squares at 2½in (6.4cm). Each strip yields 16 squares.

Feature X Blocks

Each X block has one blue/purple fabric for the cross squares and one pale grey fabric for the centre and corners. Fabric 5 is used for all side-setting triangles.

The greys and blues are paired as follows:

Fabric 3 and Fabric 9;

Fabric 6 and Fabric 4;

Fabric 7 and Fabric 10;

Fabric 8 and Fabric 12;

Fabric 11 and Fabric 13.

Side-setting Triangles From **Fabric 5** cut 6 strips 5³⁄₁₆in (13.2cm) wide and cross cut 40 squares at 5³⁄₁₆in (13.2cm). Each strip yields 7 squares. Cut each square diagonally twice to create 4 quarter-square triangles (QSTs) from each square: 160 triangles in total.

Cross Squares From each of Fabrics 3, 6, 7, 8 and 11, cut 3 strips 3⁵⁄₁₆in (8.4cm) wide and cross cut 32 squares at 3⁵⁄₁₆in (8.4cm) from each, 160 squares in total. Each strip yields 11 squares.

Centre Squares From each of Fabrics 4, 9, 10, 12 and 13, cut a strip 3⁵⁄₁₆in (8.4cm) wide and cross cut 8 squares at 3⁵⁄₁₆in (8.4cm) from each for the centre squares.

Corner Triangles Trim the remaining pieces of Fabrics 4, 9, 10, 12 and 13 to 2⅞in (7.3cm) wide and cut an additional strip 2⅞in (7.3cm) wide from each. Cross cut 16 squares at 2⅞in (7.3cm) from each fabric, 80 squares in total. Cut each square once diagonally to create 160 half-square triangles.

Border

From Fabric 14 and cutting **down the length of the fabric,** cut 4 lengths 4½in (11.4cm) wide, positioning a column of leaves centrally down each length as shown in the quilt photograph.

Trim 2 pieces to 72½in (182.9cm) for the side borders;

Trim 2 pieces to 80½in (204.5cm) long for the top and bottom borders.

Backing

Trim Fabric 15 to 88in x 88in (224cm x 224cm).

Binding

From Fabric 5 cut 9 strips 2½in (6.4cm) wide. Remove selvedges and sew end to end with 45° seams (see page 149).

MAKING THE QUILT

Using a design wall will help to place patches in the required layout.

Use ¼in (6mm) seams throughout.

Snowball Blocks

Referring to the Snowball Block Assembly Diagram, take a Fabric 1 feature square and 4 small Fabric 2 corner squares. Position a small square right sides together on each corner of the feature square and sew diagonally (a). Trim off the excess leaving a ¼in (6mm) seam allowance (b). Press seams towards the corners to finish the block (c). Make 41 snowball blocks.

Feature Blocks

Referring to the X Block Assembly Diagram, the Quilt Assembly Diagram and the quilt photograph for fabric placement, select 4 matching squares, a corresponding centre square with matching corner triangles and 4 side-setting triangles. Sew the squares and setting triangles in diagonal rows as shown in the X Block Assembly Diagram. Make 40 X blocks in total, 8 in each pair of fabrics.

X BLOCK ASSEMBLY DIAGRAM

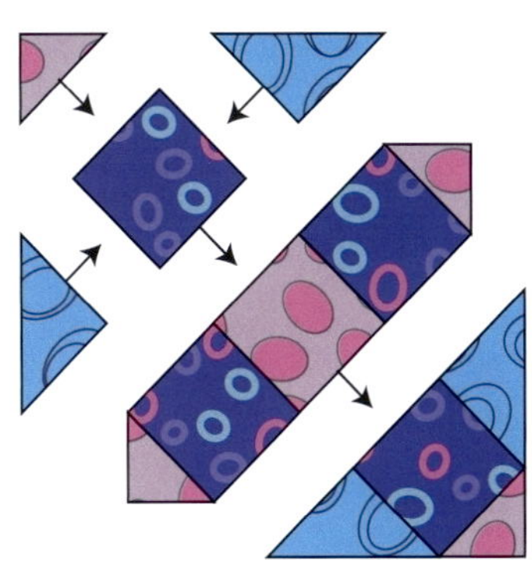

Quilt Assembly

Referring to the Quilt Assembly Diagram and the quilt photograph, lay out the blocks in 9 rows of 9 alternating snowball and feature blocks, with snowball blocks starting and ending the first and last rows. Sew the blocks together one row at a time, pressing seams in opposite directions on alternate rows – odd rows to the left, even rows to the right – to allow the finished seams to lie flat. Sew the rows together taking care to align crossing seams.

Pin then sew the shorter side borders to the quilt centre, arranging the borders so the leaf print runs in the same direction around the quilt. Press seams towards the border, then pin and sew the top and bottom borders, again checking the direction of the leaf prints around the quilt.

FINISHING THE QUILT

Press the quilt top. Layer the quilt top, batting and backing, and baste together (see page 148).

Quilt as desired and sew a button to the centre of each cross.

Trim the quilt edges and attach the binding (see page 149).

QUILT ASSEMBLY DIAGRAM

   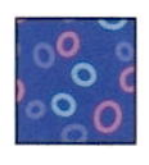 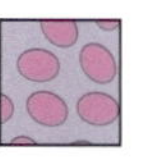

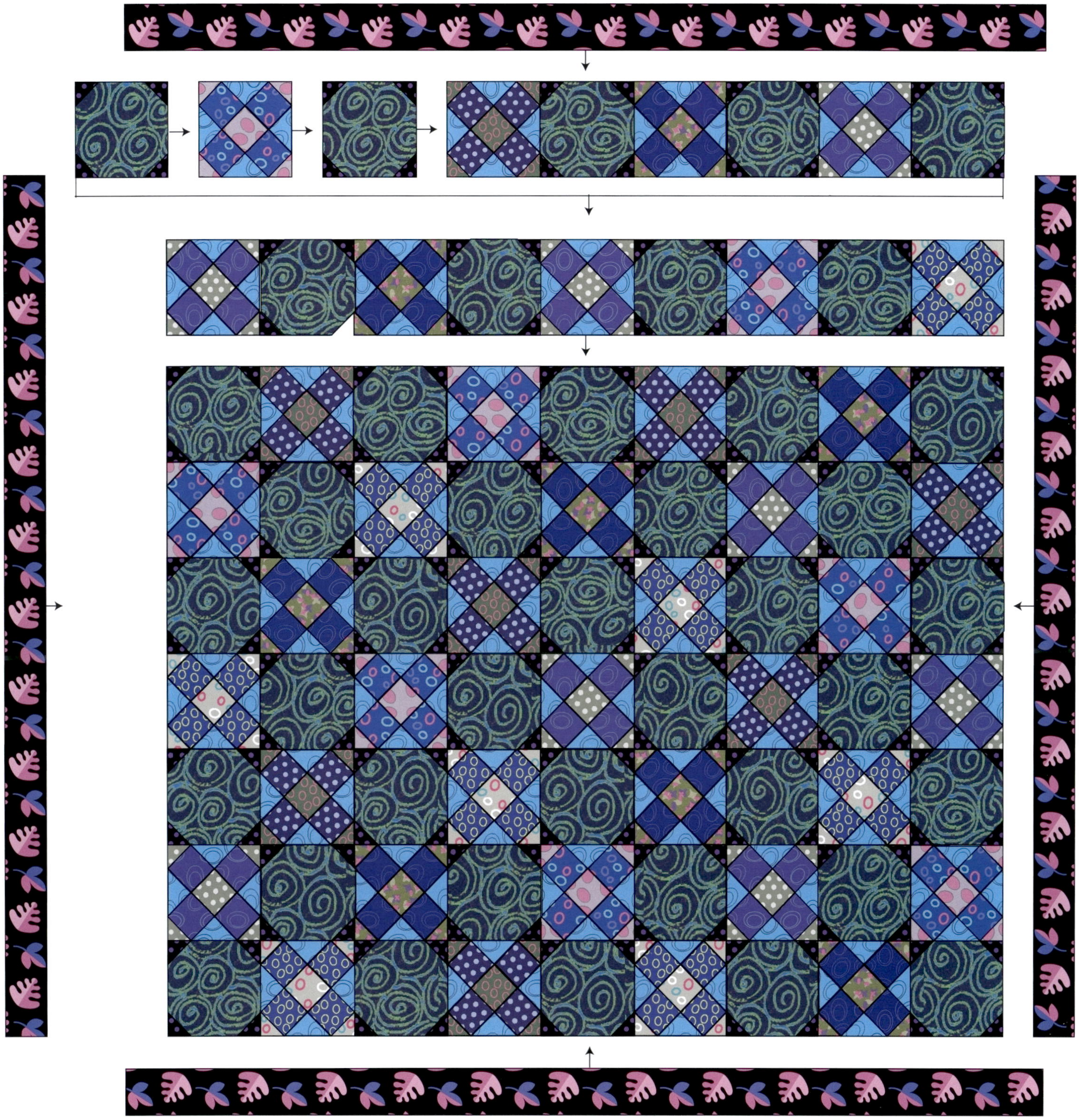

Fabric 1 Fabric 3 Fabric 5 Fabric 7 Fabric 9 Fabric 11 Fabric 13

Fabric 2 Fabric 4 Fabric 6 Fabric 8 Fabric 10 Fabric 12 Fabric 14

hot snowball circles **

Liza Prior Lucy

This snowball quilt variation features pieced circle or 'donut' blocks that are a variation of a nine-square block with a larger centre square, perfect for a feature fabric.

Follow the *Moody Snowball Criss Cross* quilt instructions on pages 92-95 but use the fabrics as listed here and shown in the Quilt Assembly Diagram. For the backing, follow the main quilt instructions but choose your own backings and bindings from the lists on page 151.

SIZE OF FINISHED QUILT

80in x 80in (203cm x 203cm)

FABRICS

Fabrics have been calculated at a maximum width of 40in (102 cm). Fabrics have been given a number – see the Fabric Swatch Diagram for details.

Patchwork Fabrics

BLOOMERS

Fabric 1 Orange 2¾yd (2.6m)

ABORIGINAL DOT

Fabric 2 Plum 1⅝yd (1.5m)

FOLK FLOWER

Fabric 3 Purple ¾yd (70cm)

ROMAN GLASS

Fabric 4 Lavender ⅜yd (40cm)

PAPERWEIGHT

Fabric 5 Blue ⅜yd (40cm)

GUINEA FLOWER

Fabric 6 Apricot ⅜yd (40cm)

Fabric 7 Moss ⅜yd (40cm)

SPOT

Fabric 8 Green ⅜yd (40cm)

Fabric 9 Melon ⅜yd (40cm)

Fabric 10 Orange ⅜yd (40cm)

GAMEBOARD

Fabric 11 Red ⅜yd (40cm)

PALM LEAVES

Fabric 12 Red 2¼yd (2.1m)

INSTRUCTIONS

Follow the cutting and making instructions for *Moody Snowball Criss Cross* on pages 92-95 for the snowball blocks and border but replace the feature block sections with the corresponding sections below.

FABRIC SWATCH DIAGRAM

Patchwork Fabrics

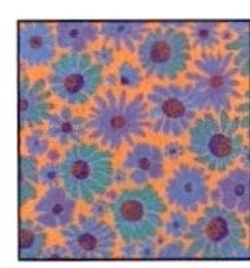

Fabric 1
BLOOMERS
Orange
BM93OR

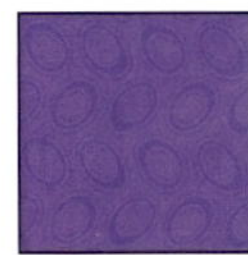

Fabric 2
ABORIGINAL DOT
Plum
GP71PL

Fabric 3
FOLK FLOWER
Purple
GP204PU

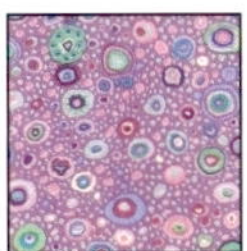

Fabric 4
ROMAN GLASS
Lavender
GP01LV

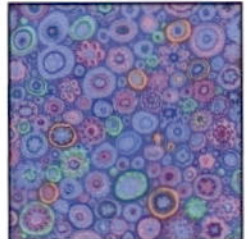

Fabric 5
PAPERWEIGHT
Blue
GP20BL

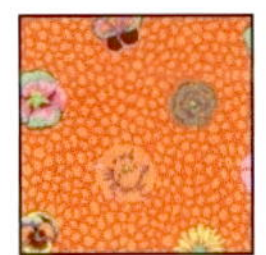

Fabric 6
GUINEA FLOWER
Apricot
GP59AP

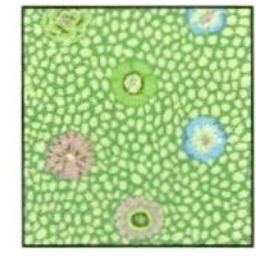

Fabric 7
GUINEA FLOWER
Moss
GP59MS

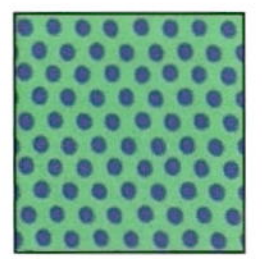

Fabric 8
SPOT
Green
GP70GN

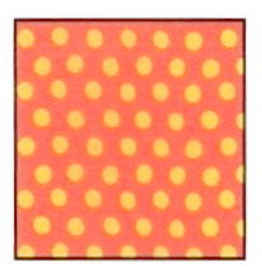

Fabric 9
SPOT
Melon
GP70ME

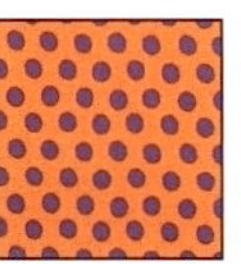

Fabric 10
SPOT
Orange
GP70OR

Fabric 11
GAMEBOARD
Red
BM95RD

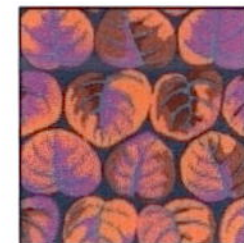

Fabric 12
PALM LEAVES
Red
GP208RD

PATCHES

The snowball blocks in all three quilts are the same size, 8in (20.3cm) finished squares, but use different fabrics.
The feature blocks in this quilt are 8in (20.3cm) finished 'donut' blocks that are also snowballs but are pieced around a central square. Patches are squares, rectangles and half-square triangles (HSTs). A centre square finished at 4in (10.2cm) is surrounded with rectangles finished 4in x 2in (10.2cm x 5.1cm) and pieced HST corner squares finished at 2in (5.1cm) square. Alternating blocks are set in 9 rows of 9 blocks and surrounded with a 4in (10.2cm) finished border.

Feature Circle Blocks

Each circle block has a Fabric 3 centre square, 4 rectangles and 4 HSTs in one of Fabrics 4-11 and 4 HSTs in Fabric 2.

Centre Squares from Fabric 3

Cut 5 strips 4½in (11.4cm) wide and cross cut 40 squares at 4½in (11.4cm). Each strip yields 8 squares.

Rectangles from each of Fabrics 4-11

Cut 2 strips 4½in (11.4cm) wide and cross cut 20 rectangles 4½in x 2½in (11.4cm x 6.4cm). Each strip yields 16 rectangles.

Corner Half-square Triangles

Trim the remaining strips of **Fabrics 4-11** from above to 2⅞in (7.3cm) wide and cross cut 10 squares at 2⅞in (7.3cm)

CIRCLE BLOCK ASSEMBLY DIAGRAM

a

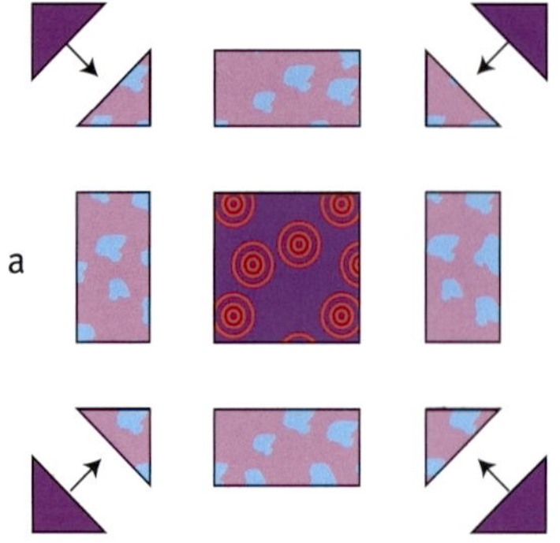

b

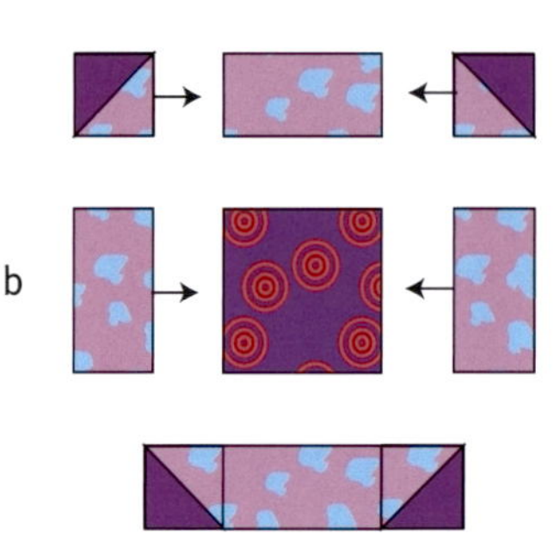

c

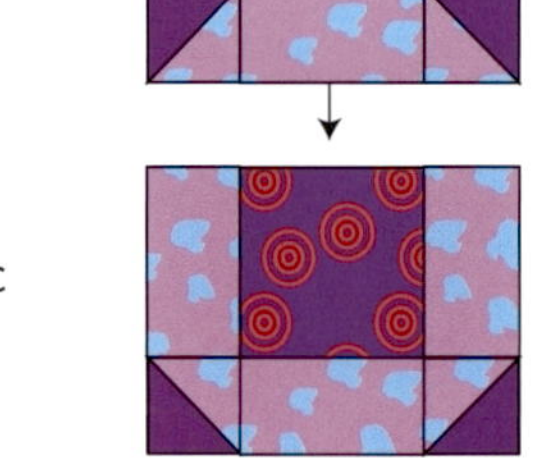

from each fabric. Cross cut each square once to create 20 HSTs from each fabric. From the remaining **Fabric 2** cut 7 strips $2\frac{7}{8}$in (7.3cm) wide and cross cut 80 squares at $2\frac{7}{8}$in (7.3cm). Each strip yields 13 squares. Cross cut each square once to create 160 HSTs.

Border

Use **Fabric 12** and follow the border cutting instructions on page 93.

MAKING THE QUILT

Snowball Blocks

Follow the instructions on page 93.

Feature Circle Blocks

Referring to the Circle Block Assembly Diagram, the Quilt Assembly Diagram and the quilt photograph for fabric placement, select a centre square, 4 matching rectangles and corner triangles and 4 Fabric 2 corner triangles. Sew sets of corner triangles together to make 4 HST squares and lay out the patches to form the block (a). Sew the squares and rectangles together to form 3 rows (b), then sew the 3 rows together to complete the block (c). Make 40 circle blocks in total, 5 in each of Fabrics 4-11.

FINISHING THE QUILT

This patchwork has been finished as a patchwork top. To prevent fraying, sew a double hem around the outer edge of the border to complete the top.

If you prefer to quilt your patchwork, cut batting and backing 8in (20.3cm) larger than the quilt top. Layer the quilt top, batting and backing, and baste together (see page 148).

Quilt as desired.

Trim the quilt edges and attach the binding (see page 149).

QUILT ASSEMBLY DIAGRAM

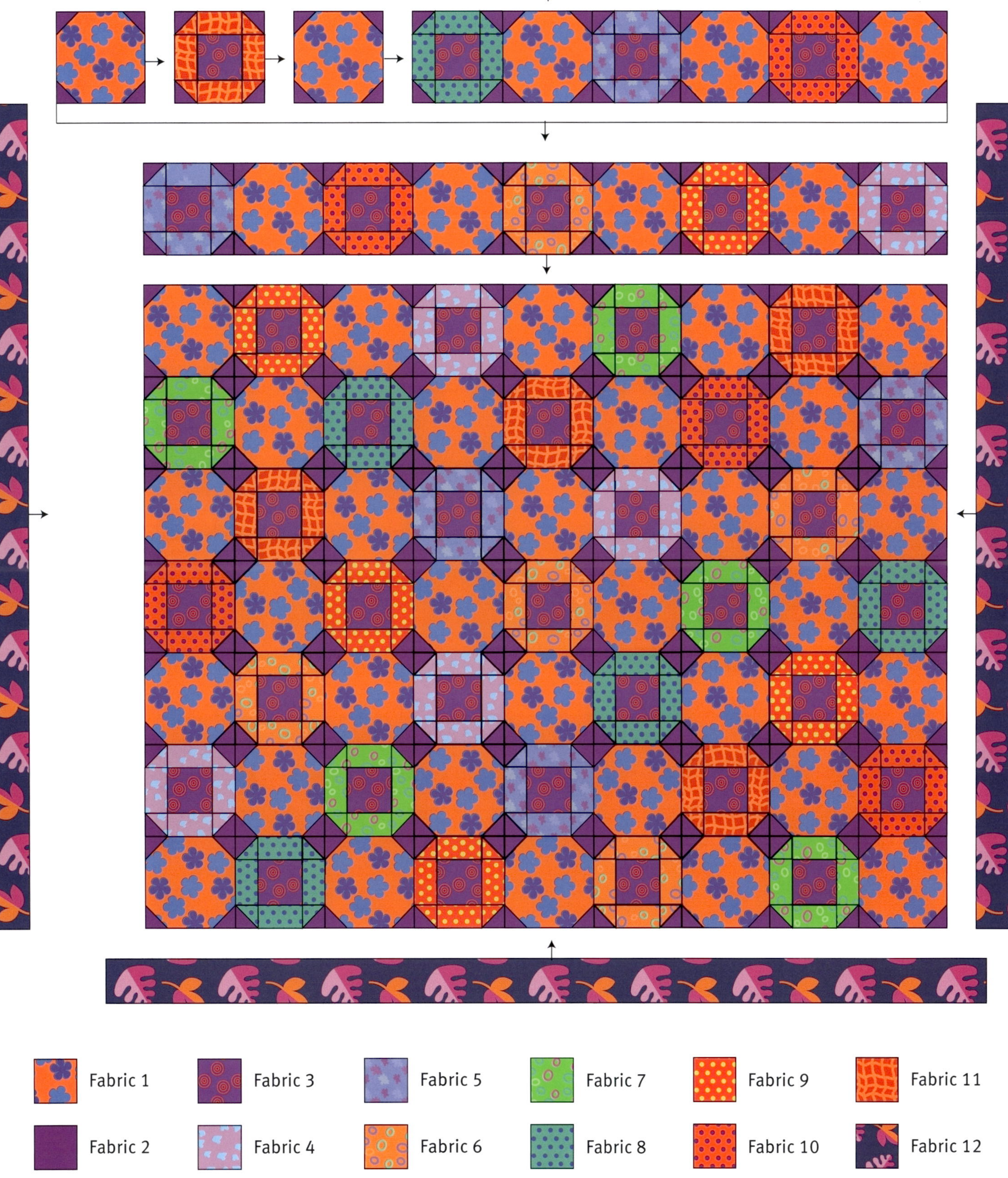

contrast snowball stars **

Liza Prior Lucy

This snowball quilt variation takes snowball blocks to the next level. The feature blocks in this version are sawtooth blocks with the addition of half-square triangle (HST) corner squares that fit together with the snowball block corners.

Follow the *Moody Snowball Criss Cross* quilt instructions on pages 92-95 but use the fabrics as listed here and shown in the Quilt Assembly Diagram. For the backing, follow the main quilt instructions but choose your own backings and bindings from the lists on page 151.

SIZE OF FINISHED QUILT
80in x 80in (203cm x 203cm)

FABRICS
Fabrics have been calculated at a maximum width of 40in (102cm). Fabrics have been given a number – see the Fabric Swatch Diagram for details.

Patchwork Fabrics

LOTUS LEAF

Fabric 1	Grey	3⅜yd (3.2m)

ABORIGINAL DOT

Fabric 2	Orchid	1yd (95cm)

SPOT

Fabric 3	Buff	1⅝yd (1.5m)
Fabric 4	Toast	⅜yd (40cm)
Fabric 5	Violet	⅜yd (40cm)
Fabric 6	Plum	½yd (50cm)

MILLEFIORE

Fabric 7	Antique	¾yd (70cm)
Fabric 8	Aqua	¾yd (70cm)
Fabric 9	Dusty	¾yd (70cm)

JAPANESE CHRYSANTHEMUM

Fabric 10	Antique	1⅛yd (1.1m)

INSTRUCTIONS
Follow the cutting and making instructions for *Moody Snowball Criss Cross* on pages 92-95 for the snowball blocks but replace the feature block and border sections with the corresponding sections below.

FABRIC SWATCH DIAGRAM

Patchwork Fabrics

Fabric 1
LOTUS LEAF
Grey
GP29GY

Fabric 2
ABORIGINAL DOT
Orchid
GP71OD

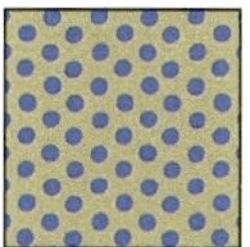

Fabric 3
SPOT
Buff
GP70BF

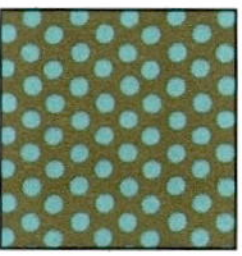

Fabric 4
SPOT
Toast
GP70TT

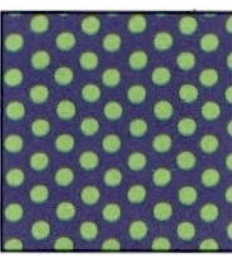

Fabric 5
SPOT
Violet
GP71VI

Fabric 6
SPOT
Plum
GP70PL

Fabric 7
MILLEFIORE
Antique
GP92AN

Fabric 8
MILLEFIORE
Aqua
GP92AQ

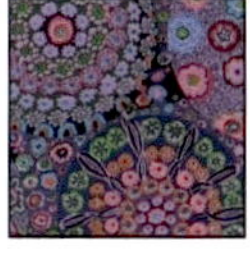

Fabric 9
MILLEFIORE
Dusty
GP92DY

Fabric 10
JAPANESE CHRYSANTHEMUM
Antique
PJ41AN

STAR BLOCK ASSEMBLY DIAGRAM

a

b

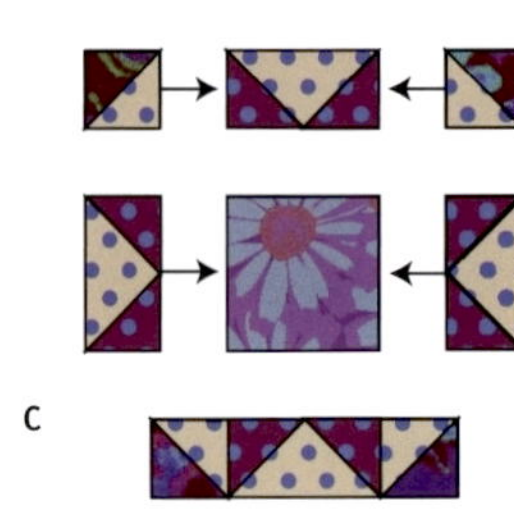
c

d

PATCHES

The snowball blocks in all three quilts are the same size, 8in (20.3cm) finished squares, but use different fabrics.

The feature blocks in this quilt are 8in (20.3cm) finished sawtooth blocks that are also snowballs because of their HST corner squares. Patches are squares, rectangles and HSTs. A centre square finished at 4in (10.2cm) is surrounded with 'flying geese' rectangles finished 4in x 2in (10.2cm x 5.1cm) and pieced HST corner squares finished at 2in (5.1cm) square. Alternating blocks are set in 9 rows of 9 blocks and surrounded with a 4in (10.2cm) finished border.

Feature – Star Blocks

Each star block has a fussy-cut centre square, 4 flying geese pieced rectangles and 4 HST corner squares. All star blocks have backgrounds in Fabric 3 and HST corners in Fabrics 1 and 3. There are three combinations for the fussy-cut centre squares and star points:

Fabrics 7 and 4;

Fabrics 8 and 5;

Fabrics 9 and 6.

Centre Squares Fussy cut 4½in (11.4cm) squares from fabrics as follows: 13 from Fabric 7, 13 from Fabric 8 and 14 from Fabric 9. Extra fabric has been allowed for fussy cutting.

Star Points From each of **Fabrics 4, 5** and **6** cut strips 2⅞in (7.3cm) wide and cross cut squares at 2⅞in (7.3cm). Each strip will yield 13 squares. Cut each square diagonally once to create 2 HSTs from each square. Cut strips, squares and triangles from fabrics as follows:

Fabric 4 (4 strips) 52 squares – 104 triangles;

Fabric 5 (4 strips) 52 squares – 104 triangles;

Fabric 6 (5 strips) 56 squares – 112 triangles.

Background – Side-setting Triangles

From **Fabric 3** cut 6 strips 5¼in (13.3cm) wide and cross cut 40 squares at 5¼in (13.3cm). Each strip yields 7 squares. Cut each square diagonally twice to create 4 quarter-square triangles (QSTs) from each square: 160 triangles in total.

Corner HST Squares From each of the remaining **Fabrics** 1 and 3 cut 7 strips 2⅞in (7.3cm) wide and cross cut 80 squares at 2⅞in (7.3cm). Each full strip will yield 13 squares. Cut each square diagonally once to create 2 HSTs from each square: 180 HSTs in total.

Border

From Fabric 10 cut 8 strips 4½in (11.4cm) wide, and sew end to end, pressing seams open. From the length:

Cut 2 pieces to 72½in (182.9cm) for the side borders;

Cut 2 pieces to 80½in (204.5cm) long for the top and bottom borders.

MAKING THE QUILT

Snowball Blocks

Follow the instructions on page 93.

Feature – Star Blocks

Select a centre square, 8 matching star point HSTs, 4 background side-setting triangles and 4 of each of the Fabric 1 and 3 HSTs for the corner squares. Referring to the Star Block Assembly Diagram, the Quilt Assembly Diagram and the quilt photograph for fabric placement, lay out the patches and sew 2 star-point triangles to each of the 4 background side-setting triangles (a). Sew each pair of Fabric 1 and 3 HSTs together to form the corner squares (b). Checking the orientation of the corner squares, sew to each side of the top and bottom triangle sections, and sew the side triangle sections to each side of the centre square (c), then sew the 3 rows together to form each star (d). Make 40 star blocks in total.

FINISHING THE QUILT

This patchwork has been finished as a patchwork top. To prevent fraying, sew a double hem around the outer edge of the border to complete the top.

If you prefer to quilt your patchwork, cut batting and backing 8in (20.3cm) larger than the quilt top. Layer the quilt top, batting and backing, and baste together (see page 148).

Quilt as desired.

Trim the quilt edges and attach the binding (see page 149).

QUILT ASSEMBLY DIAGRAM

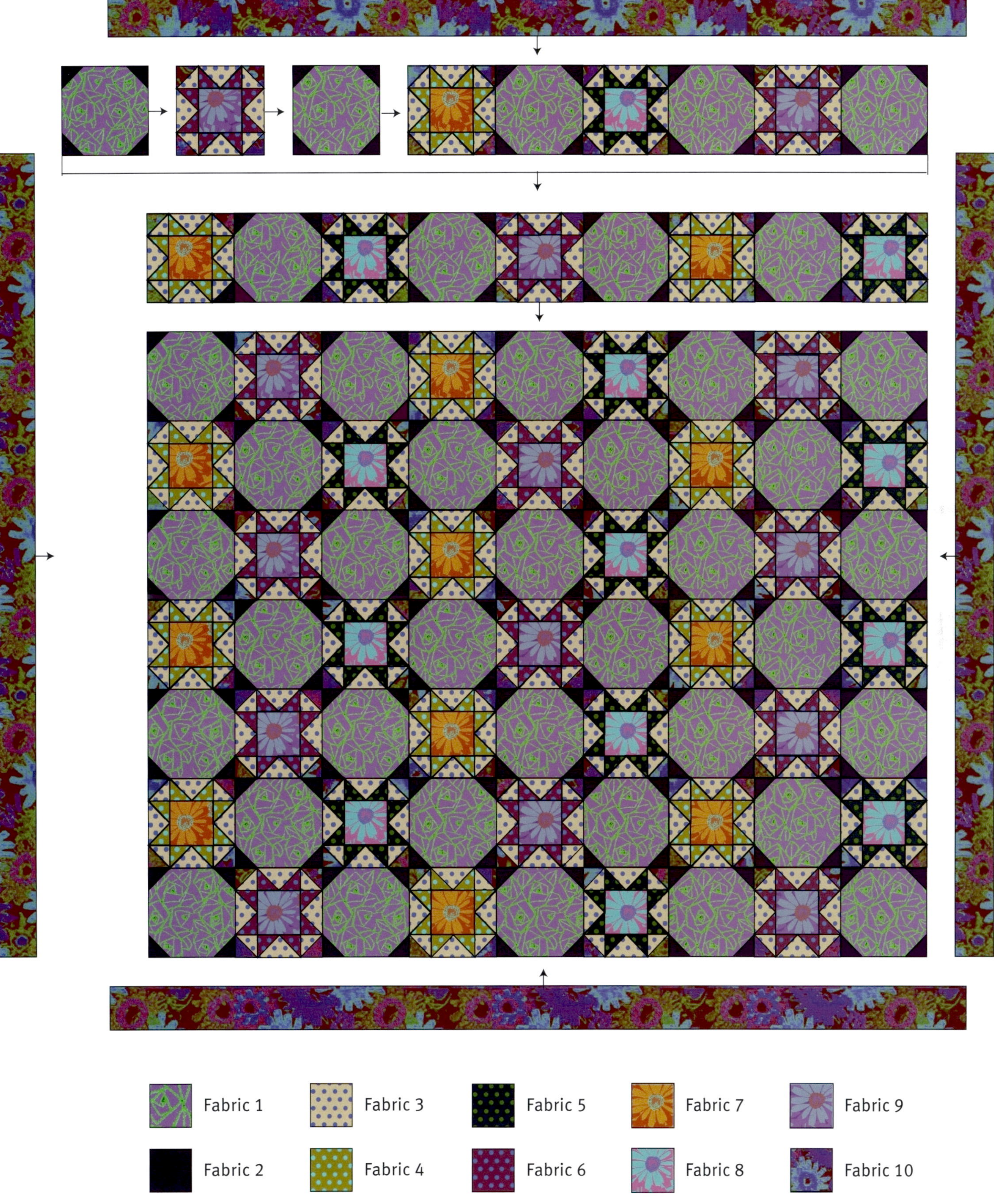

rich dark medallion *

Kaffe Fassett

Medallion quilts can range from the super simple to the extremely complicated. This one has a simple but very effective centre panel in Philip Jacobs' beautiful Gradi Floral print surrounded by concentric border prints. The double border of striking black and green hourglass blocks sets the design off perfectly.

Two alternative versions are included, each showcasing a different colour palette. The instructions for them follow the main quilt construction method but include their own fabric choices. For the backing and bindings of the alternatives, follow the main quilt instructions but choose your own backings and bindings from the lists on page 151.

SIZE OF FINISHED QUILT

60in x 54in (152.4cm x 137.2cm)

FABRICS

Fabrics have been calculated at a maximum width of 40in (102cm). Fabrics have been given a number – see Fabric Swatch Diagram for details.

Patchwork Fabrics

GRADI FLORAL
Fabric 1 Contrast 1yd (95cm)
PENNY-WISE
Fabric 2 Green ¼yd (25cm)
FLOWER STUDIES
Fabric 3 Black ⅞yd (85cm)
GAMEBOARD
Fabric 4 Magenta ⅜yd (40cm)
ABORIGINAL DOT
Fabric 5 Orchid 1¼yd (1.2m)
LOTUS LEAF
Fabric 6 Emerald 1¼yd (1.2m)

Backing and Binding Fabrics

MILLEFIORE extra-wide backing
Fabric 7 Jade 1¾yd (1.7m)

COMB STRIPE
Fabric 8 Green ⅝yd (60cm)

Batting

68in x 62in (173cm x 158cm)

PATCHES

A centre medallion is surrounded by three borders of varying widths. Each border is sewn by attaching the side borders first, followed by the top and bottom borders. The hourglass blocks in the double outer border are made from quarter-square triangles (QSTs) cut from squares, making 6in (15.2cm) finished blocks.

CUTTING OUT

Fabric is cut across the width unless otherwise stated.

Centre Panel

From Fabric 1 cut a panel, centring a floral bouquet, measuring 22½in (57.2cm) long and 16½in (41.9cm) wide.

Border 1

From Fabric 2 cut 3 strips 1½in (3.8cm) wide and cross cut pieces as follows:
2 pieces 22½in x 1½in (57.2cm x 3.8cm) for the sides;
2 pieces 18½in x 1½in (47cm x 3.8cm) for the top and bottom.

Border 2

From Fabric 3 cut 4 strips 4½in (11.4cm) wide **down the length of the fabric,** positioning a column of flowers along each piece. Trim the pieces as follows:
2 pieces 24½in x 4½in (62.2cm x 11.4cm) for the sides;
2 pieces 26½in x 4½in (67.3cm x 11.4cm) for the top and bottom.

Border 3

From Fabric 4 cut 4 strips 2½in (6.4cm) wide and cut pieces as follows:
2 pieces 32½in x 2½in (82.6cm x 6.4cm) for the sides;
2 pieces 30½in x 2½in (77.5cm x 6.4cm) for the top and bottom.

Double Hourglass Border

Cut 6 strips a scant 7¼in (18.4cm) wide from each of Fabrics 5 and 6 and cross cut squares at a scant 7¼in (18.4cm). Each strip will yield 5 squares, 30 squares in each fabric. Cross cut each square diagonally twice to yield 4 QSTs from each square, 120 in total from each fabric.

FABRIC SWATCH DIAGRAM

Patchwork Fabrics

Fabric 1
GRADI FLORAL
Contrast
PJ53CN

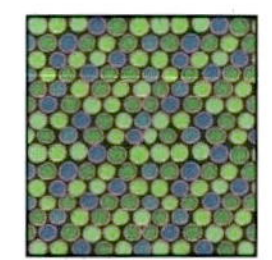

Fabric 2
PENNY-WISE
Green
GP206GN

Fabric 3
FLOWER STUDIES
Black
GP205BK

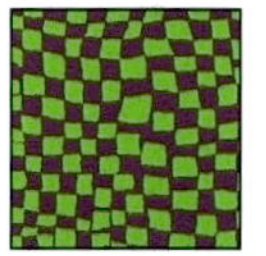

Fabric 4
GAMEBOARD
Magenta
BM95MG

Fabric 5
ABORIGINAL DOT
Orchid
GP71OD

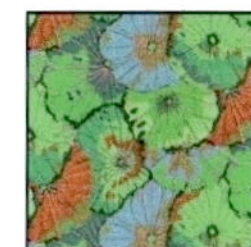

Fabric 6
LOTUS LEAF
Emerald
GP29EM

Backing and Binding Fabrics

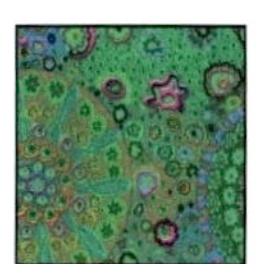

Fabric 7
MILLEFIORE
Jade
QB06JA

Fabric 8
COMB STRIPE
Green
BM84GN

BLOCK ASSEMBLY DIAGRAM

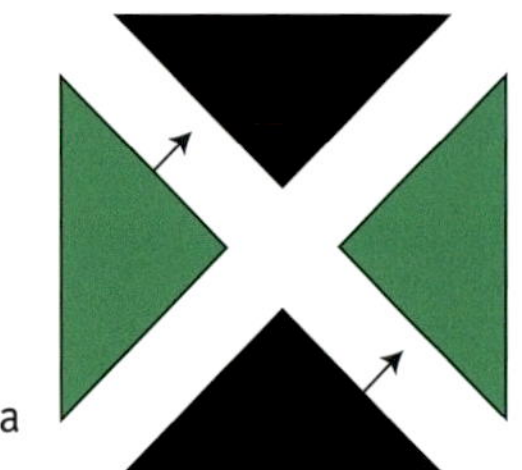

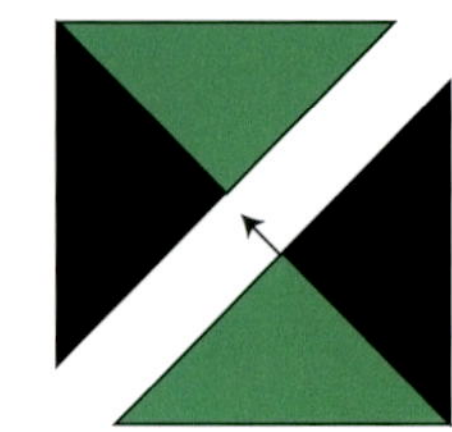

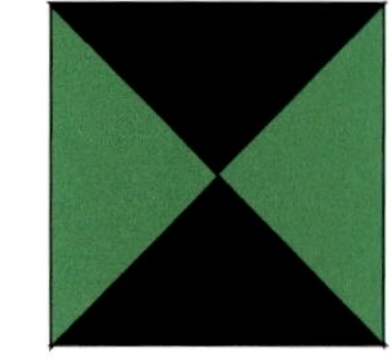

Backing
Trim Fabric 7 to 68in x 62in (173cm x 158cm).

Binding
This binding is bias cut to make the stripes diagonal. Unfold Fabric 8 and make a cut at 45° to the selvedge. From the diagonal, cut 8 strips 2½in (6.4cm) wide and sew end to end with 45° seams (see page 149).

MAKING THE QUILT
Using a design wall will help to place patches in the required layout.
Use ¼in (6mm) seams throughout.

Making the hourglass blocks
Each hourglass block is made with 4 QSTs, 2 each from Fabrics 5 and 6. Referring to the Block Assembly Diagram, sew triangles together, Fabric 5 triangles to Fabric 6 triangles (a), press seams towards the darker triangles and then sew two pairs of triangles together (b). Lightly press seam to one side of the finished block (c). Make 60 hourglass blocks.

Assembling the Quilt
Sew each border to the centre medallion in turn. Start with the side pieces, then press seams towards the borders. Next add the top and bottom pieces and again press seams toward the border. Repeat with the second and third borders.

Referring to the Quilt Assembly Diagram and quilt photograph for placement, lay out the hourglass blocks in 4 rows of 9 blocks, alternating placement of triangles on the top and bottom, with those on the sides.
Sew the blocks together one row at a time, pressing seams in opposite directions on alternate rows – odd rows to the left, even rows to the right – to allow the finished seams to lie flat. Make 4 rows, sew the 2 rows above the medallion together and then sew the 2 rows below the medallion together, taking care to align crossing seams. From the remaining blocks, make 4 columns of 6 blocks and sew each column of blocks together as with the rows, checking that the triangle placements alternate as before and that they also alternate with those in the top and bottom sections. Sew 2 columns together for each side of the medallion.

Check the layout is correct, with triangles alternating between top and bottom and sides, then pin and sew a pair of 6 block columns to each side of the medallion. Press seams towards the centre, then sew a pair of 9 block rows to the top and bottom of the medallion to complete the quilt top.

FINISHING THE QUILT
Press the quilt top. Layer the quilt top, batting and backing, and baste together (see page 148).
Quilt as desired.
Trim the quilt edges and attach the binding (see page 149).

QUILT ASSEMBLY DIAGRAM

 Fabric 1

  Fabric 2

 Fabric 3

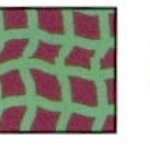 Fabric 4

 Fabric 5

 Fabric 6

rosy medallion *

Kaffe Fassett

This hot pink version of the medallion quilt uses the lavender colourway of Philip Jacobs' Gradi Floral print and my Flower Studies print in blue to give it real contrast. The instruction method is the same as that for the *Rich Dark Medallion* quilt, but with different fabrics. Follow the *Rich Dark Medallion* quilt instructions on pages 105-107 but use the fabrics as listed here and shown in the Quilt Assembly Diagram.

SIZE OF FINISHED QUILT

60in x 54in (152.4cm x 137.2cm)

FABRICS

Fabrics have been calculated at a maximum width of 40in (102cm). Fabrics have been given a number – see Fabric Swatch Diagram for details.

Patchwork Fabrics

GRADI FLORAL
Fabric 1 Lavender 1yd (95cm)
GAMEBOARD
Fabric 2 Purple 1/4yd (25cm)
FLOWER STUDIES
Fabric 3 Blue 7/8yd (85cm)
PASHA PAISLEY
Fabric 4 Black 3/8yd (40cm)
ABORIGINAL DOT
Fabric 5 Midnight 1 1/4yd (1.2m)
BRASSICA
Fabric 6 Magenta 1 1/4yd (1.2m)

INSTRUCTIONS

Follow the cutting and making instructions for the *Rich Dark Medallion* quilt on pages 105-7. The same fabric numbers are used for both quilts.

FINISHING THE QUILT

This patchwork has been finished as a patchwork top. To prevent fraying, sew a double hem around the outer edge of the border to complete the top.

If you prefer to quilt your patchwork, cut batting and backing 8in (20.3cm) larger than the quilt top. Layer the quilt top, batting and backing, and baste together (see page 148).

Quilt as desired.

Trim the quilt edges and attach the binding (see page 149).

FABRIC SWATCH DIAGRAM

Patchwork Fabrics

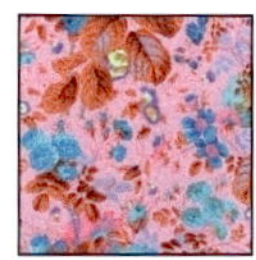

Fabric 1
GRADI FLORAL
Lavender
PJ53LV

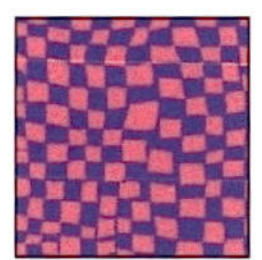

Fabric 2
GAMEBOARD
Purple
BM95PU

Fabric 3
FLOWER STUDIES
Blue
GP205BL

Fabric 4
PASHA PAISLEY
Black
BM96BK

Fabric 5
ABORIGINAL DOT
Midnight
GP71MD

Fabric 6
BRASSICA
Magenta
PJ51MG

QUILT ASSEMBLY DIAGRAM

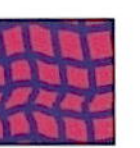 Fabric 1

 Fabric 2

 Fabric 3

 Fabric 4

Fabric 5

 Fabric 6

soft pastel medallion *

Liza Prior Lucy

Liza's soft, pastel medallion quilt is the same in format as the other versions but has an extra fabric used in the hourglass block border. The instructions are the same as for the quilt, but with different fabrics. Follow the *Rich Dark Medallion* quilt instructions on pages 105-107 but use the fabrics as listed here and shown in the Quilt Assembly Diagram.

SIZE OF FINISHED QUILT

60in x 54in (152.4cm x 137.2cm)

FABRICS

Fabrics have been calculated at a maximum width of 40in (102cm). Fabrics have been given a number – see Fabric Swatch Diagram for details.

Patchwork Fabrics

MILLEFIORE

Fabric 1	Lilac	1yd (95cm)

ABORIGINAL DOT

Fabric 2	Cantaloupe	1/4yd (25cm)

SQUARE DANCE

Fabric 3	Pastel	7/8yd (85cm)

SPOT

Fabric 4	Turquoise	3/8yd (40cm)

GUINEA FLOWER

Fabric 5	Lavender	1 1/4yd (1.2m)

PETALS

Fabric 6	Blue	3/4yd (70cm)
Fabric 7	Sky	7/8yd (85cm)

INSTRUCTIONS

Follow the cutting and making instructions for the *Rich Dark Medallion* quilt on pages 105-107 but replace the same-titled sections from it with the corresponding sections below. Fabric numbers for the centre panel and borders 1-3 are the same in both quilts.

Double Hourglass Border

Cut 6 strips a scant 7 1/4in (18.4cm) wide and cross cut squares at a scant 7 1/4in (18.4cm). Each strip will yield 5 squares, 30 squares in each fabric. Cross cut each square diagonally twice to yield 4 QSTs from each square. Cut strips, squares and QSTs from fabrics as follows:

Fabric 5 6 strips, 30 squares, 120 QSTs;
Fabric 6 3 strips, 13 squares, 52 QSTs;
Fabric 7 4 strips, 17 squares, 68 QSTs.

Assembling the Hourglass Borders

When laying out the blocks for the double hourglass border, use the Fabrics 5 and 6 blocks for the inner round and the Fabrics 5 and 7 blocks for the outer round as shown in the Quilt Assembly Diagram and quilt photograph.

FINISHING THE QUILT

This patchwork has been finished as a patchwork top. To prevent fraying, sew a double hem around the outer edge of the border to complete the top.

If you prefer to quilt your patchwork, cut batting and backing 8in (20.3cm) larger than the quilt top. Layer the quilt top, batting and backing, and baste together (see page 148).

Quilt as desired.

Trim the quilt edges and attach the binding (see page 149).

FABRIC SWATCH DIAGRAM

Patchwork Fabrics

Fabric 1
MILLEFIORE
Lilac
GP92LI

Fabric 2
ABORIGINAL DOT
Cantaloupe
GP71CA

Fabric 3
SQUARE DANCE
Pastel
GP203PT

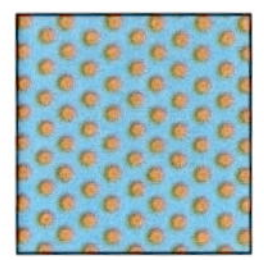

Fabric 4
SPOT
Turquoise
GP70TQ

Fabric 5
GUINEA FLOWER
Lavender
GP59LV

Fabric 6
PETALS
Blue
GP201BL

Fabric 7
PETALS
Sky
GP201SK

QUILT ASSEMBLY DIAGRAM

green economy *

Kaffe Fassett

This quilt is created using the traditional 'economy' block, popular during the Great Depression in the 1930s as it used up small scraps of fabric. It is also known as the 'square in a square' block, used here to show off our fussy-cut prints in the centre squares, while playing with contrast and colour in the surrounding triangles.

The instructions for the alternatives follow this quilt in terms of construction method but use their own fabric choices. For the backings and bindings of the alternatives, follow the main quilt instructions, but choose your own backings and bindings from the lists on page 151.

SIZE OF FINISHED QUILT

69½in x 60½in (177cm x 154cm)

FABRICS

Fabrics have been calculated at a maximum width of 40in (102cm). Fabrics have been given a number – see the Fabric Swatch Diagram for details.

Patchwork Fabrics

PASHA PAISLEY

Fabric 1	Black	¼yd (25cm)
Fabric 2	Pink	¼yd (25cm)
BLOOMERS		
Fabric 3	Grey	¼yd (25cm)
Fabric 4	Black	¼yd (25cm)
FOLK FLOWERS		
Fabric 5	Dark	¼yd (25cm)
ROMAN GLASS		
Fabric 6	Purple	⅜yd (40cm)
Fabric 7	Grey	¼yd (25cm)
AMMONITES		
Fabric 8	Dark	⅜yd (40cm)
JAPONICA		
Fabric 9	Dark	½yd (50cm)
Fabric 10	Pastel	⅜yd (40cm)
URCHIN		
Fabric 11	Pastel	⅜yd (40cm)
GUINEA FLOWER		
Fabric 12	Moss	¼yd (25cm)
SNOW FLOWER		
Fabric 13	Green	¼yd (25cm)
PAPAVER		
Fabric 14	Grey	⅜yd (40cm)
Fabric 15	Green	¼yd (25cm)
JUMBLE		
Fabric 16	Sea Foam	⅝yd (60cm)
JUNGLE		
Fabric 17	Brown	1⅝yd (1.5m)

FABRIC SWATCH DIAGRAM

Patchwork Fabrics

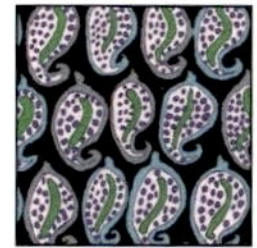

Fabric 1
PASHA PAISLEY
Black
BM96BK

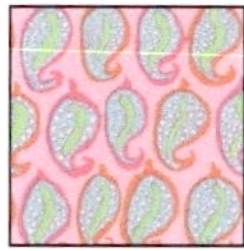

Fabric 2
PASHA PAISLEY
Pink
BM96PK

Fabric 3
BLOOMERS
Grey
BM93GY

Fabric 4
BLOOMERS
Black
BM93BK

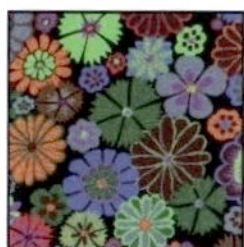

Fabric 5
FOLK FLOWERS
Dark
GP204DK

Fabric 6
ROMAN GLASS
Purple
GP01PU

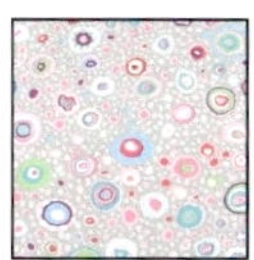

Fabric 7
ROMAN GLASS
Grey
GP01GY

Fabric 8
AMMONITES
Dark
PJ128DK

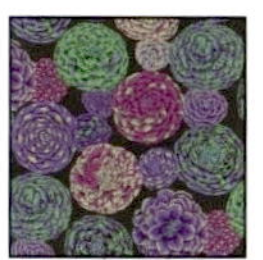

Fabric 9
JAPONICA
Dark
PJ130DK

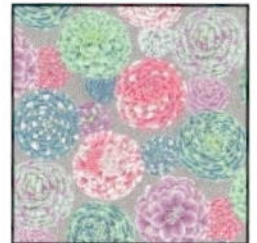

Fabric 10
JAPONICA
Pastel
PJ130PT

Fabric 11
URCHIN
Pastel
PJ125PT

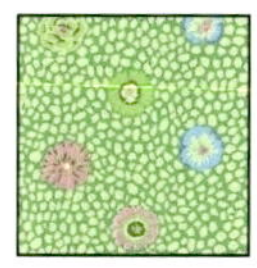

Fabric 12
GUINEA FLOWER
Moss
GP59MS

Fabric 13
SNOW FLOWER
Green
BM94GN

Fabric 14
PAPAVER
Grey
PJ127GY

Fabric 15
PAPAVER
Green
PJ127GN

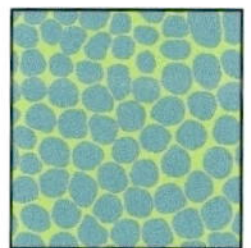

Fabric 16
JUMBLE
Sea Foam
BM53SE

Fabric 17
JUNGLE
Brown
PJ126BR

Backing and Binding Fabrics

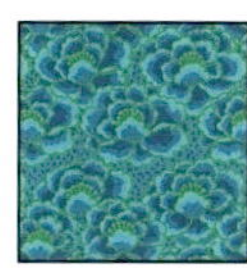

Fabric 18
TONAL FLORAL
Turquoise
QB09TQ

Fabric 19
COMB STRIPE
Pink
BM84PK

Backing and Binding Fabrics
TONAL FLORAL extra-wide backing

Fabric 18	Turquoise	2yd (1.9m)

COMB STRIPE

Fabric 19	Pink	⅝yd (60cm)

Batting
78in x 69in (198cm x 175cm)

PATCHES
Patches are made from central fussy-cut squares and half-square triangles (HSTs) forming the surrounding squares to make 9in (22.9cm) finished blocks. All triangles are cut from squares cut across the width of fabric. Blocks are set in 5 rows of 4 and surrounded by a 3in (7.6cm) finished small-print border and a 9in (22.9cm) finished large-scale print border. Note that a darker centre square has lighter inner triangles and darker outer triangles to create good contrast. This is reversed for half of the blocks that have a lighter centre square, darker inner triangles and lighter outer triangles.

CUTTING OUT
Fabric is cut across the width unless otherwise stated.
When cutting different pieces from the same fabric, always cut the larger pieces first. In this instance, cut the fussy-cut squares before cutting strips for the triangles. For best results when cutting bias-edged pieces, use spray starch before cutting.

Central Fussy-cut Squares
Fussy cut 5in (12.7cm) squares centring a bloom in each square. Cut a total of 20 squares from fabrics as follows:
Fabric 8 2 squares;
Fabric 9 8 squares;
Fabric 10 5 squares;
Fabric 11 2 squares;
Fabric 14 2 squares;
Fabric 15 1 square.

Outer Triangles
Cut a strip 5⅜in (13.7cm) wide from each fabric below and cross cut squares at 5⅜in (13.7cm). Each strip yields 7 squares. Cut each square once diagonally to make a total of 80 triangles. Cut squares and triangles as follows:

BLOCK ASSEMBLY DIAGRAM

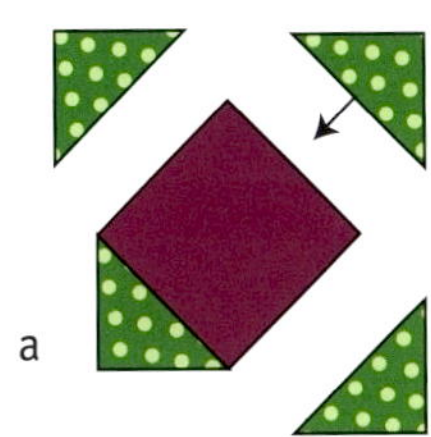

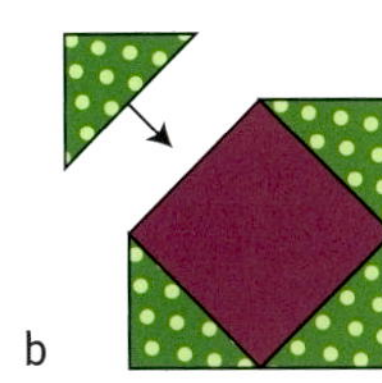

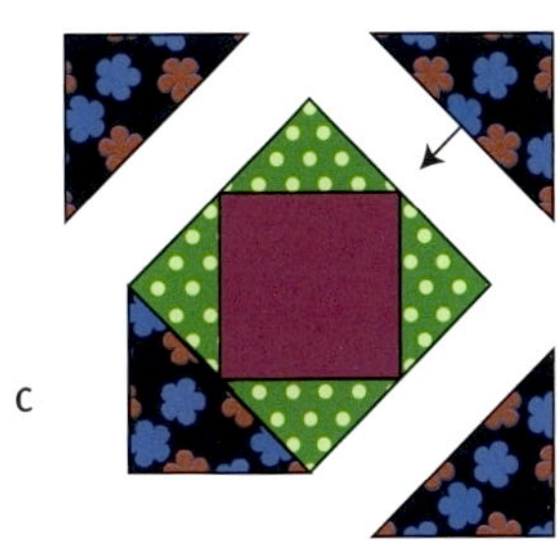

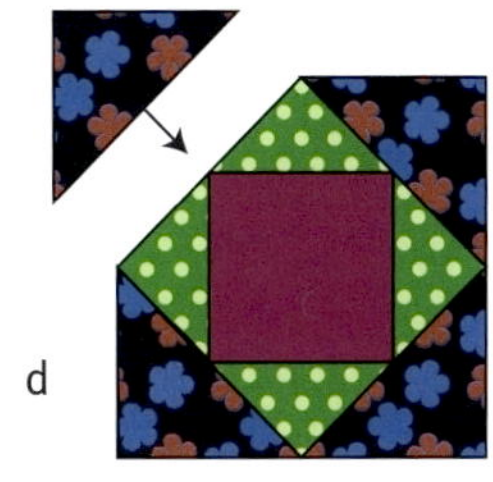

Fabric 1 4 squares – 8 triangles;
Fabric 2 2 squares – 4 triangles;
Fabric 3 4 squares – 8 triangles;
Fabric 4 4 squares – 8 triangles;
Fabric 5 2 squares – 4 triangles;
Fabric 6 4 squares – 8 triangles;
Fabric 8 2 squares – 4 triangles;
Fabric 11 4 squares – 8 triangles;
Fabric 13 4 squares – 8 triangles;
Fabric 14 6 squares –12 triangles;
Fabric 15 4 squares – 8 triangles.

Inner Triangles

Trim remaining strips from above to 4in (10.2cm) wide and, if required, cut an additional strip 4in (10.2cm) wide. Cross cut squares at 4in (10.2cm). Each full strip yields 10 squares. Cut each square once diagonally to make a total of 80 triangles. Cut squares and triangles as follows:
Fabric 1 2 squares – 4 triangles;
Fabric 2 4 squares – 8 triangles;
Fabric 4 4 squares – 8 triangles;
Fabric 5 4 squares – 8 triangles;
Fabric 6 (+ 1 strip) 6 squares – 12 triangles;
Fabric 7 (+ 1 strip) 4 squares – 8 triangles;
Fabric 8 4 squares – 8 triangles;
Fabric 11 2 squares – 4 triangles;
Fabric 12 (+ 1 strip) 6 squares – 12 triangles;
Fabric 13 4 squares – 8 triangles.

Border 1

From Fabric 16 cut 5 strips 3½in (8.9cm) wide. Join strips end to end using ¼in (6mm) seams, and press seams open. From the length, cut border pieces as follows:
2 pieces 45½in x 3½in (115.6cm x 8.9cm) for the side borders;
2 pieces 42½in x 3½in (108cm x 8.9cm) for the top and bottom borders.

Border 2

From Fabric 17 cut 6 strips 9½in (24.1cm) wide. Join strips end to end using ¼in (6mm) seams, and press seams open. From the length, cut border pieces as follows:
2 pieces 51½in x 9½in (130.8cm x 24.1cm) for the side borders;
2 pieces 60½in x 9½in (153.7cm x 24.1cm) for the top and bottom borders.

Backing

Trim Fabric 18 to 78in x 69in (198cm x 175cm).

Binding

From Fabric 19 cut 7 strips 2½in (6.4cm) wide. Remove selvedges and sew end to end with 45° seams (see page 149).

MAKING THE QUILT

Using a design wall will help to place patches in the required layout.
Use ¼in (6mm) seams throughout.

Making the Blocks

Referring to the Block Assembly Diagram and the quilt photograph, sew inner triangles to opposite sides of a centre square (a), then sew inner triangles to the remaining 2 sides (b). Repeat the process, sewing outer triangles to opposite sides (c), then complete the block by sewing outer triangles to the remaining 2 sides (d). Make 20 blocks measuring 9½in (24.1cm) square, easing if necessary.

Lay out the blocks referring to the Quilt Assembly Diagram and the quilt photograph. Note that the blocks alternate in tone between those with lighter inner triangles and darker outer triangles and those with darker inner triangles and lighter outer triangles, playing the contrasts against each other. Sew the blocks together one row at a time, pressing seams in opposite directions on alternate rows – odd rows to the left, even rows to the right – to allow the finished seams to lie flat. Sew the rows together taking care to align crossing seams.

Borders

Pin (to prevent stretching) and sew the longer Border 1 pieces to each side of the centre, press seams towards the border, then pin and sew the top and bottom Border 1 pieces to the centre, again pressing seams towards the border. Repeat with the Border 2 side pieces, then the Border 2 top and bottom pieces to complete the quilt top.

FINISHING THE QUILT

Press the quilt top. Layer the quilt top, batting and backing, and baste together (see page 148).
Quilt as desired.
Trim the quilt edges and attach the binding (see page 149).

QUILT ASSEMBLY DIAGRAM

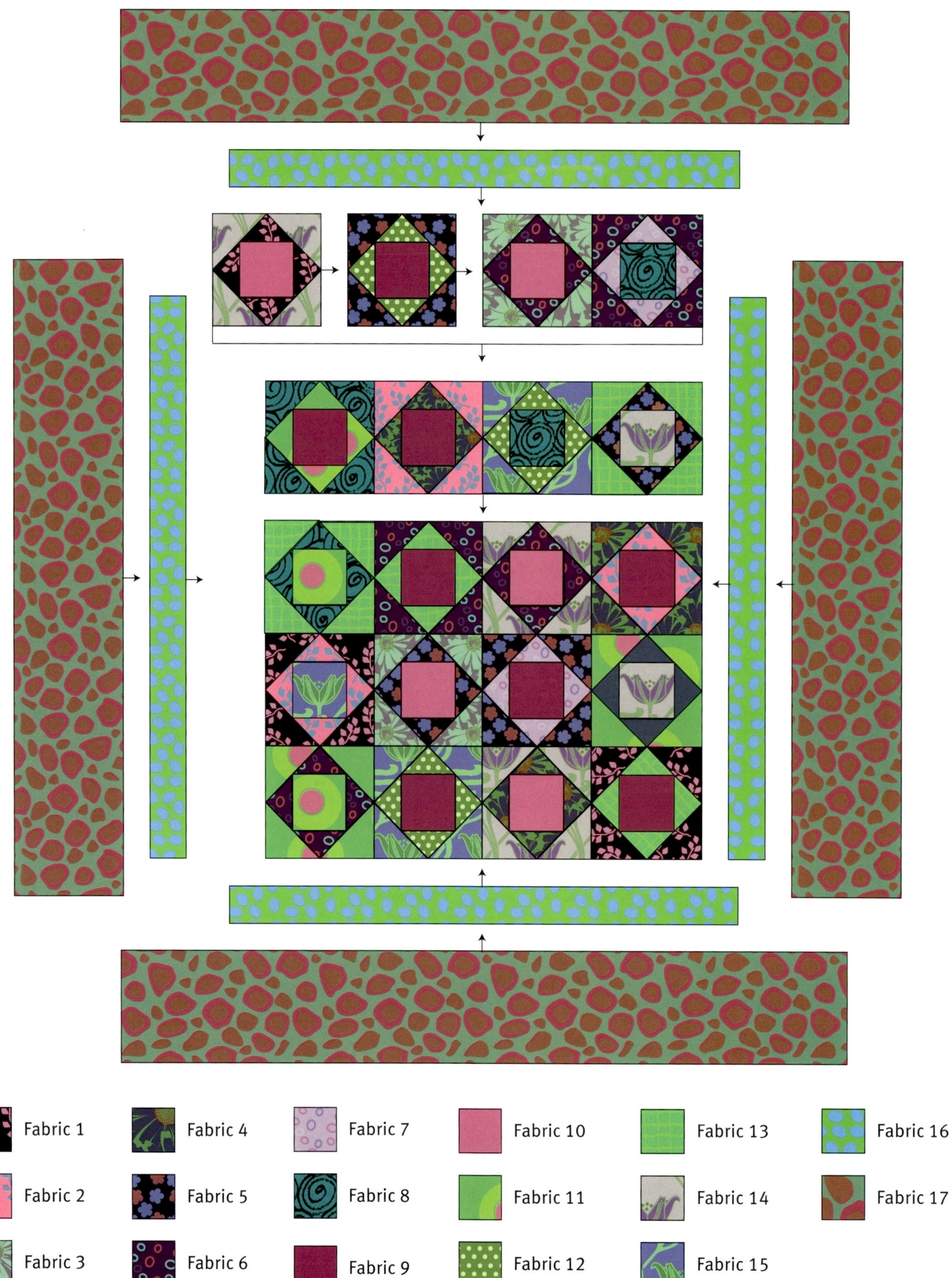

hot economy *

Kaffe Fassett

This bright version of the economy quilt shows off some beautiful fabrics in hot reds and pinks along with some contrasts in the fussy-cut blooms as well as the smaller prints.

Follow the *Green Economy* quilt instructions on pages 115-118 but use the fabrics as listed here and shown in the Quilt Assembly Diagram.

SIZE OF FINISHED QUILT

69½in x 60½in (177cm x 154cm)

FABRICS

Fabrics have been calculated at a maximum width of 40in (102cm). Fabrics have been given a number – see the Fabric Swatch Diagram for details.

Patchwork Fabrics

JAPONICA

Fabric 1	Contrast	½yd (50cm)

PAPAVER

Fabric 2	Red	½yd (50cm)
Fabric 3	Orange	½yd (50cm)

CACTUS FLOWER

Fabric 4	Red	¼yd (25cm)

URCHIN

Fabric 5	Red	¼yd (25cm)

AMMONITES

Fabric 6	Pink	¼yd (25cm)

GUINEA FLOWER

Fabric 7	Red	⅜yd (40cm)

FOLK FLOWER

Fabric 8	Pink	¼yd (25cm)
Fabric 9	Red	⅛yd (15cm)
Fabric 10	Purple	¼yd (25cm)

SPOT

Fabric 11	Melon	¼yd (25cm)
Fabric 12	Royal	⅛yd (15cm)

PASHA PAISLEY

Fabric 13	Blue	¼yd (25cm)
Fabric 14	Purple	¼yd (25cm)
Fabric 15	Aqua	¼yd (25cm)

GAMEBOARD

Fabric 16	Purple	¼yd (25cm)
Fabric 17	Pink	¼yd (25cm)

JUMBLE

Fabric 18	Bubblegum	¼yd (25cm)

MILLEFIORE

Fabric 19	Pink	⅛yd (15cm)

SNOW FLOWER

Fabric 20	Pink	¾yd (70cm)

GRADI FLORAL

Fabric 21	Tomato	1⅝yd (1.5m)

FABRIC SWATCH DIAGRAM

Patchwork Fabrics

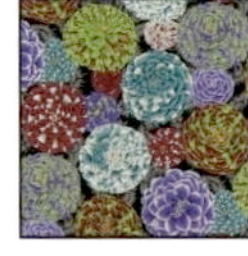

Fabric 1
JAPONICA
Contrast
PJ130CN

Fabric 2
PAPAVER
Red
PJ127RD

Fabric 3
PAPAVER
Orange
PJ127OR

Fabric 4
CACTUS FLOWER
Red
PJ96RD

Fabric 5
URCHIN
Red
PJ125RD

Fabric 6
AMMONITES
Pink
PJ128PK

Fabric 7
GUINEA FLOWER
Red
GP59RD

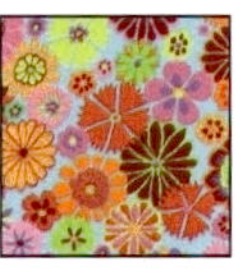

Fabric 8
FOLK FLOWER
Pink
GP204PK

Fabric 9
FOLK FLOWER
Red
GP204RD

Fabric 10
FOLK FLOWER
Purple
GP204PU

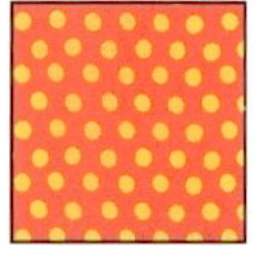

Fabric 11
SPOT
Melon
GP70ME

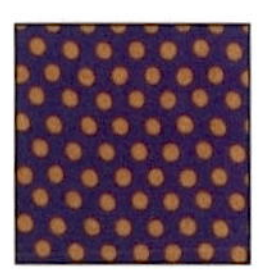

Fabric 12
SPOT
Royal
GP70RY

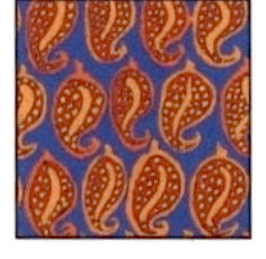

Fabric 13
PASHA PAISLEY
Blue
BM96BL

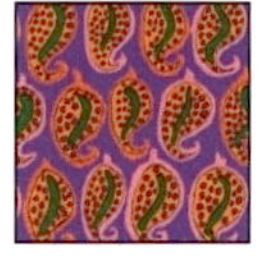

Fabric 14
PASHA PAISLEY
Purple
BM96PU

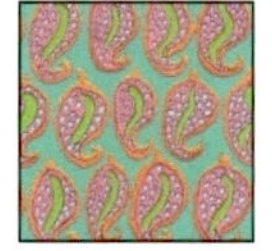

Fabric 15
PASHA PAISLEY
Aqua
BM96AQ

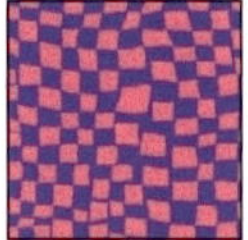

Fabric 16
GAMEBOARD
Purple
BM95PU

Fabric 17
GAMEBOARD
Pink
BM95PK

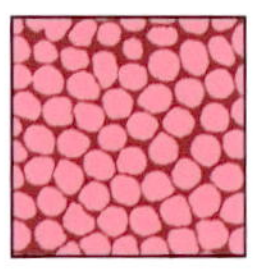

Fabric 18
JUMBLE
Bubblegum
BM53BB

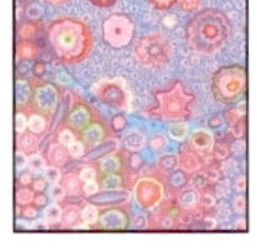

Fabric 19
MILLEFIORE
Pink
GP92PK

Fabric 20
SNOW FLOWER
Pink
BM94PK

Fabric 21
GRADI FLORAL
Tomato
PJ53TM

INSTRUCTIONS
Follow the cutting and making instructions for the *Green Economy* quilt on pages 115-118 but replace the same-titled sections from it with the corresponding sections below.

CUTTING OUT
Fabric is cut across the width unless otherwise stated. When cutting different pieces from the same fabric, always cut the larger pieces first. In this instance, cut the fussy-cut squares before cutting strips for the triangles. For best results, when cutting bias edged pieces use spray starch before cutting.

Central Fussy-cut Squares
Fussy cut 5in (12.7cm) squares centring a bloom in each square. Cut a total of 20 squares from fabrics as follows:
Fabric 1 10 squares;
Fabric 2 2 squares;
Fabric 3 3 squares;
Fabric 4 3 squares;
Fabric 5 1 square;
Fabric 6 1 square.

Outer Triangles
Cut a strip 5⅜in (13.7cm) wide from each fabric below and cross cut squares at 5⅜in (13.7cm). Each strip will yield 7 squares. Cut each square once diagonally to make a total of 80 triangles. Cut squares and triangles as follows:
Fabric 2 2 squares – 4 triangles;
Fabric 3 2 squares – 4 triangles;
Fabric 6 2 squares – 4 triangles;
Fabric 7 6 squares – 12 triangles;
Fabric 8 4 squares – 8 triangles;
Fabric 10 2 squares – 4 triangles;
Fabric 11 2 squares – 4 triangles;
Fabric 13 2 squares – 4 triangles;
Fabric 14 4 squares – 8 triangles;
Fabric 15 4 squares – 8 triangles;
Fabric 16 2 squares – 4 triangles;
Fabric 17 2 squares – 4 triangles;
Fabric 18 4 squares – 8 triangles;
Fabric 20 2 squares – 4 triangles.

Inner Triangles
Trim remaining strips from above to 4in (10.2cm) wide and, if required, cut an additional strip 4in (10.2cm) wide. Cross cut squares at 4in (10.2cm). Each full strip yields 8 squares. Cut each square

once diagonally to make a total of 80 triangles. Cut squares and triangles as follows:

Fabric 5 2 squares – 4 triangles;
Fabric 7 (+ 1 strip) 2 squares – 4 triangles;
Fabric 8 2 squares – 4 triangles;
Fabric 9 2 squares – 4 triangles;
Fabric 11 6 squares – 12 triangles;
Fabric 12 6 squares – 12 triangles;
Fabric 14 2 squares – 4 triangles;
Fabric 15 2 squares – 4 triangles;
Fabric 16 4 squares – 8 triangles;
Fabric 17 2 squares – 4 triangles;
Fabric 18 4 squares – 8 triangles;
Fabric 19 4 squares – 8 triangles;
Fabric 20 2 squares – 4 triangles.

Border 1
Use Fabric 20 and follow instructions on page 117.
From Fabric 20 cut 5 strips 3½in (8.9cm) wide. Join strips end to end using ¼in (6mm) seams, and press seams open. From the length cut border pieces as follows:
2 pieces 45½in x 3½in (115.6cm x 8.9cm) for the side borders;
2 pieces 42½in x 3½in (108cm x 8.9cm) for the top and bottom borders.

Border 2
Use Fabric 21 and follow instructions on page 117.
From Fabric 21 cut 6 strips 9½in (24.1cm) wide. Join strips end to end using ¼in (6mm) seams, and press seams open. From the length cut border pieces as follows:
2 pieces 51½in x 9½in (130.8cm x 24.1cm) for the side borders;
2 pieces 60½in x 9½in (153.7cm x 24.1cm) for the top and bottom borders.

MAKING THE QUILT

Using a design wall will help to place patches in the required layout.
Use ¼in (6mm) seams throughout.

Making the Blocks
Referring to the Block Assembly Diagram on page 117 and the quilt photograph, sew inner triangles to opposite sides of a centre square (a), then sew inner triangles to the remaining 2 sides (b). Repeat the process, sewing outer triangles to opposite sides (c), then complete the block sewing outer triangles to the remaining 2 sides (d). Make 20 blocks measuring 9½in (24.1cm) square, easing if necessary.

Lay out the blocks referring to the Quilt Assembly Diagram and the quilt photograph for fabric placement. Sew together one row at a time, pressing seams in opposite directions on alternate rows – odd rows to the left, even rows to the right – to allow the finished seams to lie flat. Sew the rows together taking care to align crossing seams.

Borders
Pin (to prevent stretching borders) and sew the longer Border 1 pieces to the centre, press seams towards the border, then pin and sew the top and bottom Border 1 pieces to the centre, again pressing seams towards the Border. Repeat with the Border 2 side pieces, then the Border 2 top and bottom to complete the quilt top.

FINISHING THE QUILT

This patchwork has been finished as a patchwork top. To prevent fraying, sew a double hem around the outer edge of the border to complete the top.
If you prefer to quilt your patchwork, cut batting and backing 8in (20.3cm) larger than the quilt top. Layer the quilt top, batting and backing, and baste together (see page 148).
Quilt as desired.
Trim the quilt edges and attach the binding (see page 149).

QUILT ASSEMBLY DIAGRAM

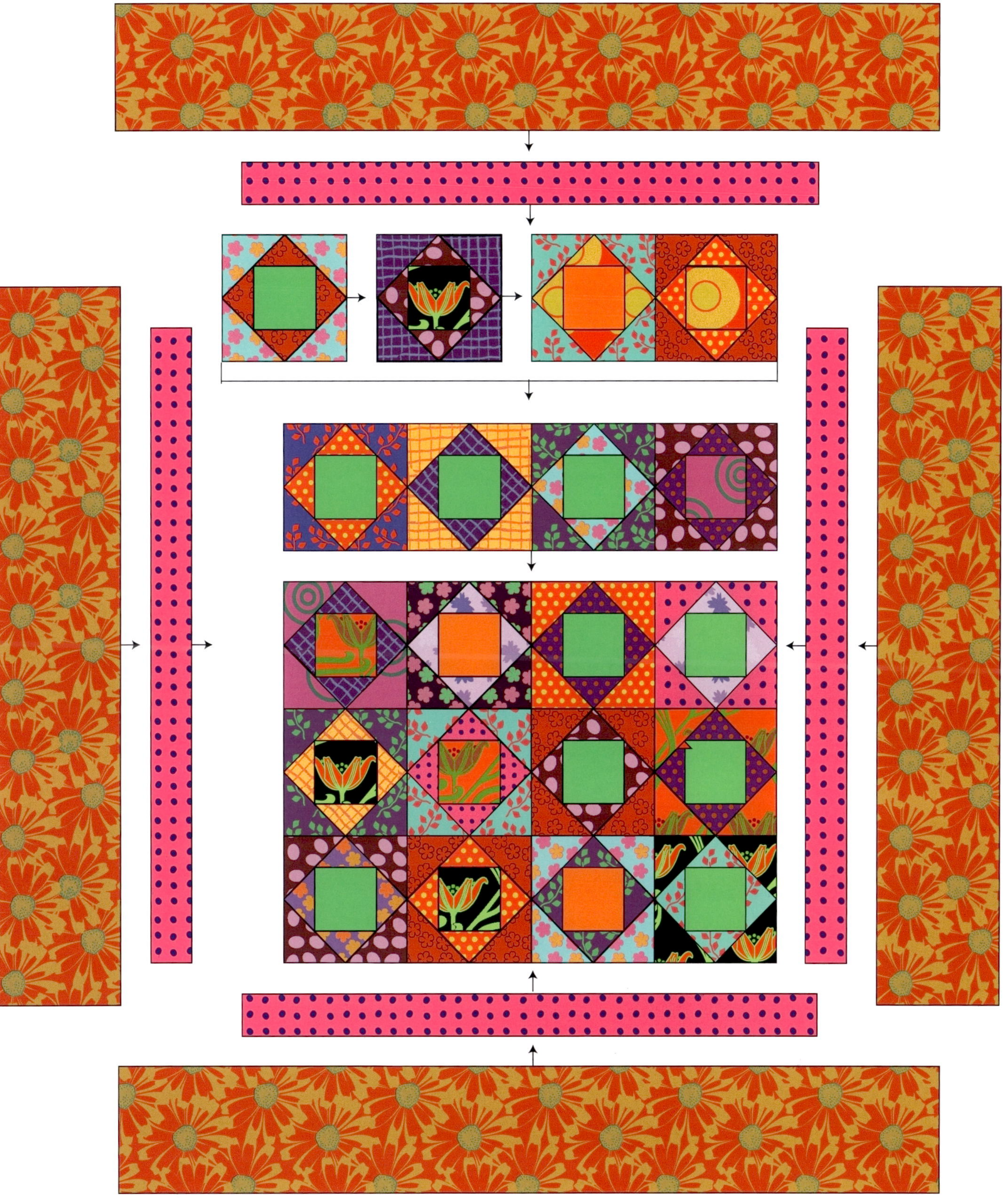

cool economy *

Kaffe Fassett

This delicious berry-blue version of the economy quilt really showcases the use of contrasting tones in a chosen colour palette. Brandon's Checkmate print in Blue is perfect for the border.

Follow the *Green Economy* quilt instructions on pages 115-118 but use the fabrics as listed here and shown in the Quilt Assembly Diagram.

SIZE OF FINISHED QUILT

$69\frac{1}{2}$in x $60\frac{1}{2}$in (177cm x 154cm)

FABRICS

Fabrics have been calculated at a maximum width of 40in (102cm). Fabrics have been given a number – see the Fabric Swatch Diagram for details.

Patchwork Fabrics

JAPONICA		
Fabric 1	Blue	1yd (95cm)
ROMAN GLASS		
Fabric 2	Lavender	$\frac{1}{4}$yd (25cm)
PAPERWEIGHT		
Fabric 3	Blue	$\frac{1}{4}$yd (25cm)
Fabric 4	Purple	$\frac{1}{4}$yd (25cm)
SPOT		
Fabric 5	Storm	$\frac{1}{4}$yd (25cm)
Fabric 6	Indigo	$\frac{1}{4}$yd (25cm)
ABORIGINAL DOT		
Fabric 7	Plum	$\frac{1}{4}$yd (25cm)
Fabric 8	Periwinkle	$\frac{1}{4}$yd (25cm)
MILLEFIORE		
Fabric 9	Aqua	$\frac{1}{4}$yd (25cm)
Fabric 10	Blue	$\frac{1}{4}$yd (25cm)
PETALS		
Fabric 11	Blue	$\frac{1}{4}$yd (25cm)
JUMBLE		
Fabric 12	Duck Egg	$\frac{5}{8}$yd (60cm)
CHECKMATE		
Fabric 13	Blue	$1\frac{3}{4}$yd (1.7m)

INSTRUCTIONS

Follow the cutting and making instructions for the *Green Economy* quilt on pages 115-118 but replace the same-titled sections from it with the corresponding sections below.

Central Fussy-cut Squares

From Fabric 1 fussy cut 5in (12.7cm) squares centring a bloom in each square. Cut a total of 20 squares, 10 from the paler blooms and 10 from the darker blooms.

FABRIC SWATCH DIAGRAM

Patchwork Fabrics

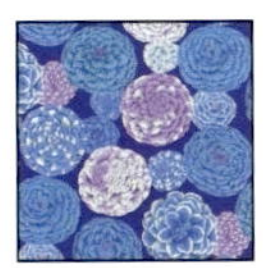

Fabric 1
JAPONICA
Blue
PJ130BL

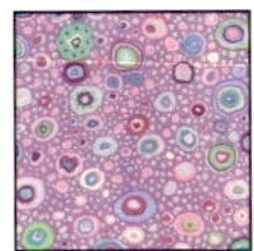

Fabric 2
ROMAN GLASS
Lavender
GP01LV

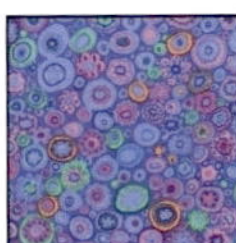

Fabric 3
PAPERWEIGHT
Blue
GP20BL

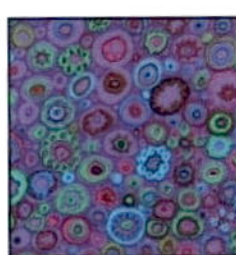

Fabric 4
PAPERWEIGHT
Purple
GP20PU

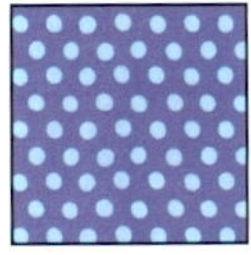

Fabric 5
SPOT
Storm
GP70SR

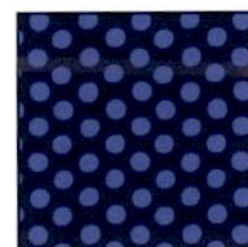

Fabric 6
SPOT
Indigo
GP70IN

Fabric 7
ABORIGINAL DOT
Plum
GP71PL

Fabric 8
ABORIGINAL DOT
Periwinkle
GP71PE

Fabric 9
MILLEFIORE
Aqua
GP92AQ

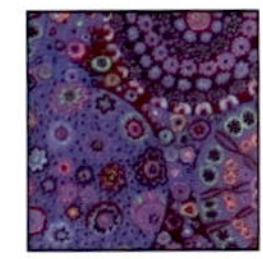

Fabric 10
MILLEFIORE
Blue
GP92BL

Fabric 11
PETALS
Blue
GP201BL

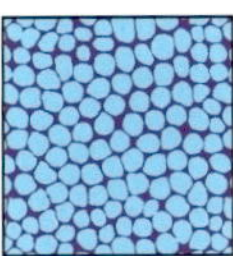

Fabric 12
JUMBLE
Duck Egg
BM53DE

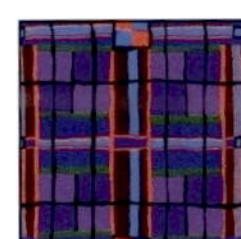

Fabric 13
CHECKMATE
Blue
BM86BL

Outer Triangles

From each of **Fabrics 2-11**, cut a strip $5\frac{3}{8}$in (13.7cm) wide and cross cut 4 squares at $5\frac{3}{8}$in (13.7cm) from each fabric. Cut each square once diagonally to make 8 triangles from each fabric, a total of 80 outer triangles.

Inner Triangles

Trim each remaining strip of **Fabrics 2-11** from above to 4in (10.2cm) wide and cross cut 4 squares from each fabric at 4in (10.2cm). Cut each square once diagonally to make 8 triangles from each fabric, a total of 80 inner triangles.

Border 1

Use Fabric 12 and follow instructions on page 117.

From Fabric 12 cut 5 strips $3\frac{1}{2}$in (8.9cm) wide. Join strips end to end using $\frac{1}{4}$in (6mm) seams, and press seams open. From the length cut border pieces as follows:

2 pieces $45\frac{1}{2}$in x $3\frac{1}{2}$in (115.6cm x 8.9cm) for the side borders;

2 pieces $42\frac{1}{2}$in x $3\frac{1}{2}$in (108cm x 8.9cm) for the top and bottom borders.

Border 2
From Fabric 13 cutting **down the length of the fabric**, cut 4 border pieces 9½in (24.1cm) wide, matching up the strips into 2 pairs with similarly positioned stripes and trim to the following lengths:
2 pieces 51½in x 9½in (130.8cm x 24.1cm) for the side borders;
2 pieces 60½in x 9½in (153.7cm x 24.1cm) for the top and bottom borders.

MAKING THE QUILT
Using a design wall will help to place patches in the required layout.
Use ¼in (6mm) seams throughout.

Making the Blocks
Referring to the Block Assembly Diagram on page 117 and the quilt photograph, sew inner triangles to opposite sides of a centre square (a), then sew inner triangles to the remaining 2 sides (b). Repeat the process, sewing outer triangles to opposite sides (c) then complete the block sewing outer triangles to the remaining 2 sides (d). Make 20 blocks measuring 9½in (24.1cm) square, easing if necessary.

Lay out the blocks referring to the Quilt Assembly Diagram and the quilt photograph for fabric placement. Sew together one row at a time, pressing seams in opposite directions on alternate rows – odd rows to the left, even rows to the right – to allow the finished seams to lie flat. Sew the rows together taking care to align crossing seams.

Borders
Pin (to prevent stretching borders) and sew the longer Border 1 pieces to the centre, press seams towards the border, then pin and sew the top and bottom Border 1 pieces to the centre, again pressing seams towards the border. Repeat with the Border 2 side pieces, then the Border 2 top and bottom to complete the quilt top.

FINISHING THE QUILT
This patchwork has been finished as a patchwork top. To prevent fraying, sew a double hem around the outer edge of the border to complete the top.

If you prefer to quilt your patchwork, cut batting and backing 8in (20.3cm) larger than the quilt top. Layer the quilt top, batting and backing, and baste together (see page 148).
Quilt as desired.
Trim the quilt edges and attach the binding (see page 149).

Fabric 1
Fabric 2
Fabric 3
Fabric 4
Fabric 5
Fabric 6
Fabric 7
Fabric 8
Fabric 9
Fabric 10
Fabric 11
Fabric 12
Fabric 13

QUILT ASSEMBLY DIAGRAM

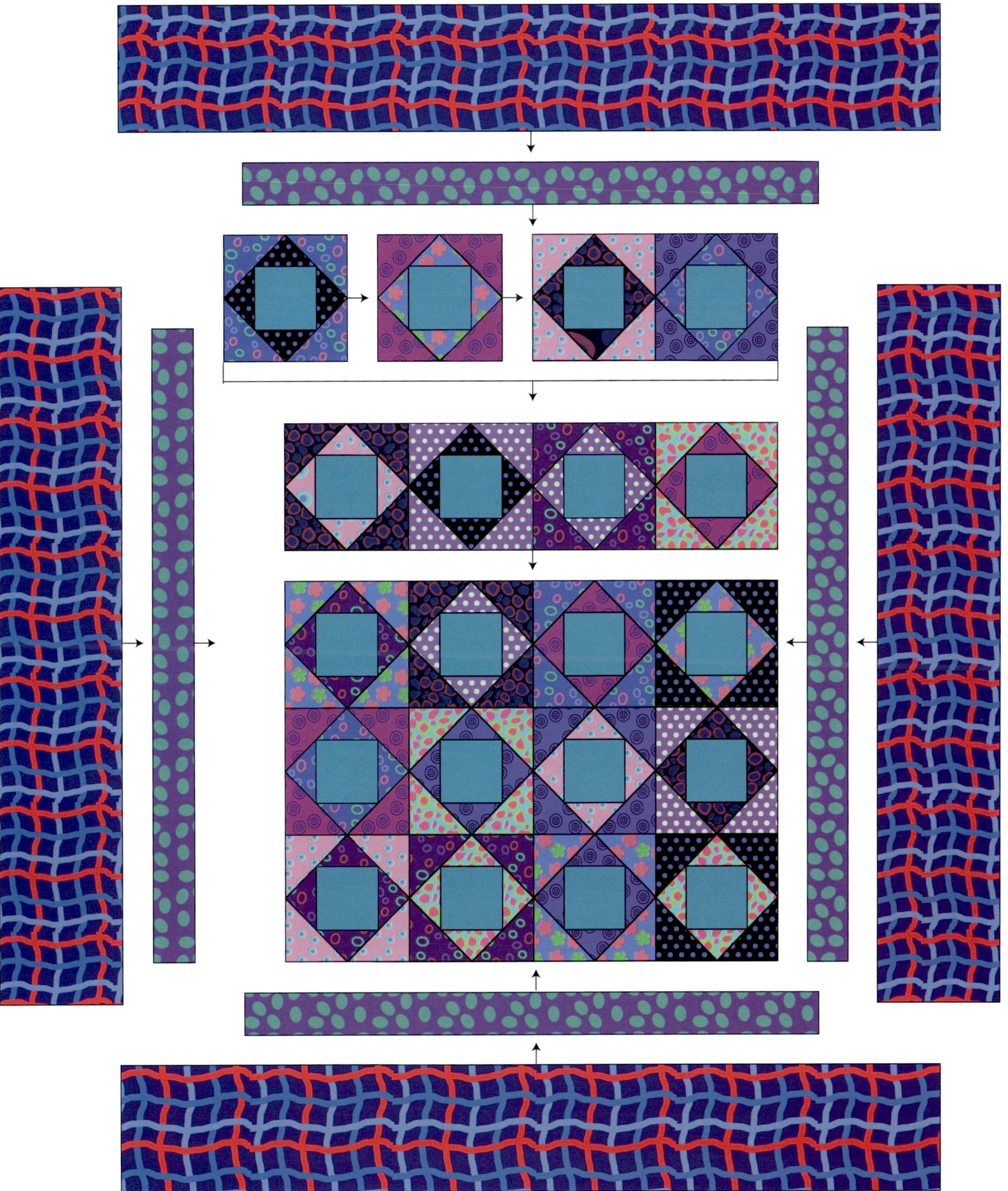

contrast chevron stripes *

Kaffe Fassett

My latest collection of Woven Stripes is perfect for this bold layout, brought together with a border in one of my woven shot cottons. This version focuses on the contrast of hot and cold colours, blending a selection of stripes in each of the colour groups.

A second version is included, showcasing a different colour palette. The instructions for the second version follow the main quilt in terms of construction method but use alternative fabric choices.

SIZE OF FINISHED QUILT

72in x 72in (183cm x 183cm)

FABRICS

Fabrics have been calculated at a maximum width of 40in (102cm). Fabrics have been given a number – see the Fabric Swatch Diagram for details.

Patchwork Fabrics

Blues

CATERPILLAR STRIPE

Fabric 1	Aqua	5/8yd (60cm)
Fabric 2	Dark	5/8yd (60cm)

BROAD STRIPE

Fabric 3	Azure	5/8yd (60cm)
Fabric 4	Blue	5/8yd (60cm)

EXOTIC STRIPE

Fabric 5	Denim	5/8yd (60cm)
Fabric 6	Teal	5/8yd (60cm)

Reds

CATERPILLAR STRIPE

Fabric 7	Earth	5/8yd (60cm)

NARROW STRIPE

Fabric 8	Sunset	5/8yd (60cm)
Fabric 9	Tomato	5/8yd (60cm)
Fabric 10	Wine	5/8yd (60cm)

BROAD STRIPE

Fabric 11	Red	5/8yd (60cm)

EXOTIC STRIPE

Fabric 12	Warm	5/8yd (60cm)

SHOT COTTON

Fabric 13	Shadow	1 1/4yd (1.2m)

* see also Binding Fabric

Backing and Binding Fabrics

MILLEFIORE extra-wide backing

Fabric 14	Blue	2 1/4yd (2.1m)

SHOT COTTON

Fabric 13	Shadow	5/8yd (60cm)

* see also Patchwork Fabrics

FABRIC SWATCH DIAGRAM

Patchwork Fabrics

Fabric 1
CATERPILLAR STRIPE
Aqua
WS01AQ

Fabric 2
CATERPILLAR STRIPE
Dark
WS01DK

Fabric 3
BROAD STRIPE
Azure
WS03AZ

Fabric 4
BROAD STRIPE
Blue
WS03BL

Fabric 5
EXOTIC STRIPE
Denim
WS04DM

Fabric 6
EXOTIC STRIPE
Teal
WS04TE

Fabric 7
CATERPILLAR STRIPE
Earth
WS01ER

Fabric 8
NARROW STRIPE
Sunset
WS02SS

Fabric 9
NARROW STRIPE
Tomato
WS02TM

Fabric 10
NARROW STRIPE
Wine
WS02WN

Fabric 11
BROAD STRIPE
Red
WS03RD

Fabric 12
EXOTIC STRIPE
Warm
WS04WM

Fabric 13
SHOT COTTON
Shadow
SC108

Backing and Binding Fabrics

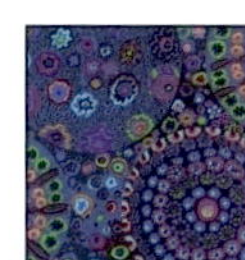

Fabric 14
MILLEFIORE
Blue
QB06BL

Fabric 13
SHOT COTTON
Shadow
SC108

DIAMOND CUTTING DIAGRAM

Method 1

Method 2

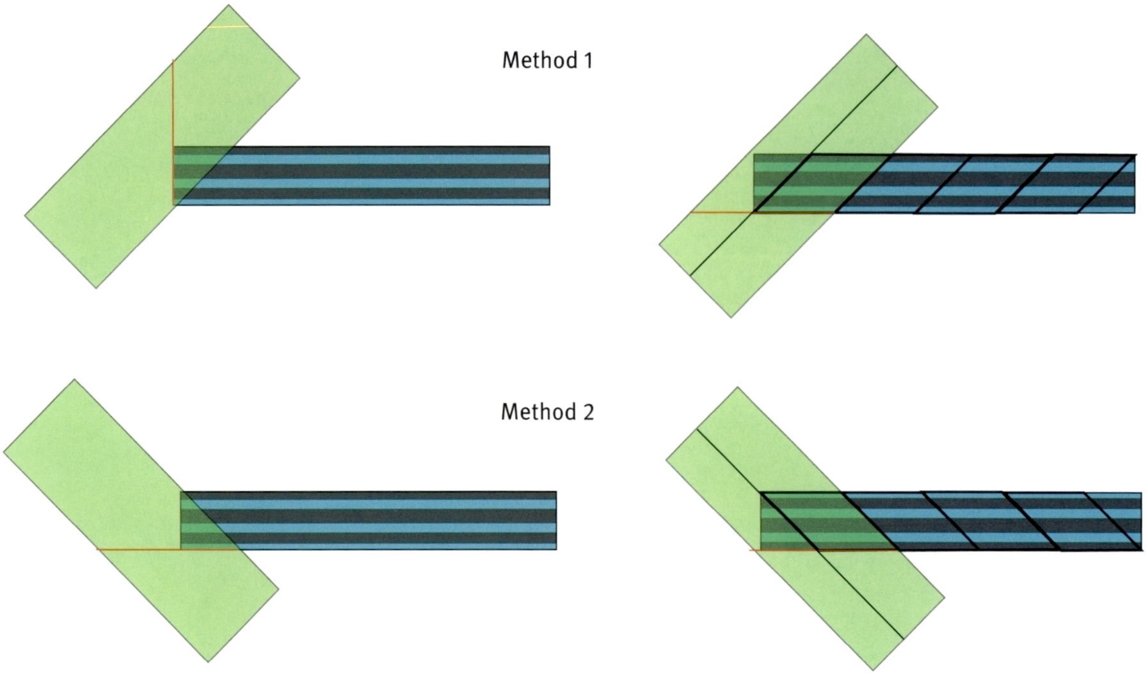

Batting
80in x 80in (204cm x 204cm)

PATCHES
Patches are 45° diamonds cut from strips cut **along the length of striped fabrics** in 2 colour groups – in this instance, blues and reds. Patches are sewn together in vertical columns and finished at each end with setting triangles. Columns are sewn together and the quilt is finished with a 3in (7.6cm) finished border. This is a scrappy design so do not try to place the fabrics exactly as in the original. Just keep the colour groups separate so that each vertical pieced column is made of only one colour group.

CUTTING OUT
Kaffe's Woven Stripes run down the length of fabric, therefore strips are cut down the length to follow the line of the stripes, but don't get overly careful about cutting exactly along the stripes. Because these fabrics are handwoven, they will not be perfectly straight. We recommend using some spray starch on the yardage before cutting.

Stripe Diamonds
From each of Woven Stripe **Fabrics 1-12**, cutting down the length, along the stripes, cut 8 strips 3½in (8.9cm) wide. Referring to the Diamond Cutting Diagram, line up the fabric with the 45° ruler marking and cut a 45° angle at one end using Method 1. Line up the 3½in (8.9cm) line with the 45° angle cut and cross-cut diamonds at 3½in (8.9cm), sliding the ruler along after every cut to make 3 diamonds from each strip. Cut the first and all odd numbered strips using Method 1 and cut the second and all even numbered strips using Method 2, so that you can match up pairs of diamonds with stripes that meet to form the chevron design.

Border and Column Ends
From **Fabric 13** cut 7 strips 3½in (8.9cm) wide. Join strips end to end using ¼in (6mm) seams, and press seams open. From the length cut pieces as follows: 2 pieces 66½in x 3½in (168.9cm x 8.9cm) for the side borders; 2 pieces 72½in x 3½in (184.2cm x 8.9cm) for the top and bottom borders. From the remaining **Fabric 13** cut 3 strips 3⅞in (9.8cm) wide and cross cut 22 squares at 3⅞in (9.8cm). Each strip will yield 10 squares. Cut each square in half diagonally once to yield 44 half-square triangles (HSTs) for the column ends.

Backing
Trim **Fabric 14** to 80in (204cm) square.

Binding
From **Fabric 13** cut 8 strips 2½in (6.4cm) wide. Remove selvedges and sew end to end with 45° seams (see page 149).

MAKING THE QUILT
Using a design wall will help to place patches in the required layout. Use ¼in (6mm) seams throughout.

Making the Chevron Stripe Columns
For each column, select 12 pairs of diamonds (1 right-leaning and 1 left-leaning) from one colour group – 2 pairs from each fabric. Lay them out in a random order as 2 columns with corresponding right- and left-leaning diamonds next to each other. Sew 12 right-leaning diamonds together, starting and ending with a Fabric 13 HST. Then sew the 12 corresponding left-leaning diamonds together in the same sequence, beginning and ending with a Fabric 13 HST. Lightly press all right-leaning diamond columns upwards and press all left-leaning diamond columns

downwards. This will help to flatten the finished seams. Sew the two columns together taking care to align the crossing seams. Make 6 red arrow columns and 5 blue arrow columns.

Assembling the Quilt

Referring to the Quilt Assembly Diagram, lay out the arrow columns in alternate colours, starting and ending with a red column. Pin (to prevent stretching) then sew the columns together taking care to align crossing seams.

Pin and sew the side borders to the centre and press seams towards the border, then pin and sew the top and bottom borders to the centre to complete the quilt top.

FINISHING THE QUILT

Press the quilt top. Layer the quilt top, batting and backing, and baste together (see page 148).

Quilt as desired.

Trim the quilt edges and attach the binding (see page 149).

QUILT ASSEMBLY DIAGRAM

russet chevron stripes *

Kaffe Fassett

This version of Chevron Stripes, while still focusing on the contrast of warmer golds and cooler greens and aquas, is more subtly toned in earthy hues from my Woven Stripe range.

Follow the *Contrast Chevron Stripes* quilt instructions on pages 129-132 but use the fabrics as listed here and shown in the Quilt Assembly Diagram. For the backing and binding, follow the main quilt instructions but choose your own backings and bindings from the lists on page 151.

SIZE OF FINISHED QUILT

72in x 72in (183cm x 183cm)

Patchwork Fabrics

Golds

CATERPILLAR STRIPE		
Fabric 1	Earth	5/8yd (60cm)
Fabric 2	Sunshine	5/8yd (60cm)
BROAD STRIPE		
Fabric 3	Dusky	5/8yd (60cm)
Fabric 4	Gold	5/8yd (60cm)
EXOTIC STRIPE		
Fabric 5	Desert	5/8yd (60cm)
Fabric 6	Warm	5/8yd (60cm)

Greens

CATERPILLAR STRIPE		
Fabric 7	Dark	5/8yd (60cm)
NARROW STRIPE		
Fabric 8	Multi	5/8yd (60cm)
BROAD STRIPE		
Fabric 9	Azure	5/8yd (60cm)
Fabric 10	Multi	5/8yd (60cm)
EXOTIC STRIPE		
Fabric 11	Khaki	5/8yd (60cm)
Fabric 12	Teal	5/8yd (60cm)
SHOT COTTON		
Fabric 13	Peppercorn	1 1/4yd (1.2m)

INSTRUCTIONS

Follow the cutting and making instructions for *Contrast Chevron Stripes* on pages 129-132 but replace the same-titled section from it with the corresponding section below.

Making the Chevron Stripe Columns

Following the instructions for *Contrast Chevron Stripes* on page 130, make 6 gold arrow columns and 5 green arrow columns.

FABRIC SWATCH DIAGRAM

Patchwork Fabrics

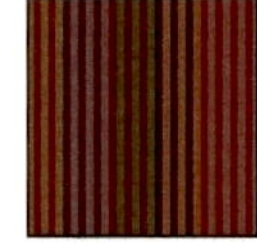

Fabric 1
CATERPILLAR STRIPE
Earth
WS01ER

Fabric 2
CATERPILLAR STRIPE
Sunshine
WS01SN

Fabric 3
BROAD STRIPE
Dusky
WS03DU

Fabric 4
BROAD STRIPE
Gold
WS03GD

Fabric 5
EXOTIC STRIPE
Desert
WS04DT

Fabric 6
EXOTIC STRIPE
Warm
WS04WM

Fabric 7
CATERPILLAR STRIPE
Dark
WS01DK

Fabric 8
NARROW STRIPE
Multi
WS02MU

Fabric 9
BROAD STRIPE
Azure
WS03AZ

Fabric 10
BROAD STRIPE
Multi
WS03MU

Fabric 11
EXOTIC STRIPE
Khaki
WS04KH

Fabric 12
EXOTIC STRIPE
Teal
WS04TE

Fabric 13
SHOT COTTON
Peppercorn
SC141PR

FINISHING THE QUILT

This patchwork has been finished as a patchwork top. To prevent fraying, sew a double hem around the outer edge of the border to complete the top.

If you prefer to quilt your patchwork, cut batting and backing 8in (20.3cm) larger than the quilt top. Layer the quilt top, batting and backing, and baste together (see page 148).

Quilt as desired.

Trim the quilt edges and attach the binding (see page 149).

QUILT ASSEMBLY DIAGRAM

leafy triangles and stripes *

Kaffe Fassett

My collection of earthy Woven Stripes looks very much at home in its partnership with this beautiful green shot cotton, resembling pennant flags, and embedded in the rich peat-coloured border.

SIZE OF FINISHED QUILT
68in x 52in (174cm x 133cm)

FABRICS
Fabrics have been calculated at a maximum width of 40in (102cm). Fabrics have been given a number – see the Fabric Swatch Diagram for details.

Patchwork Fabrics

EXOTIC STRIPE		
Fabric 1	Denim	½yd (50cm)
Fabric 2	Desert	½yd (50cm)
Fabric 3	Khaki	½yd (50cm)
Fabric 4	Midnight	½yd (50cm)
Fabric 5	Teal	½yd (50cm)
Fabric 6	Warm	½yd (50cm)
SHOT COTTON		
Fabric 7	Khaki	1⅜yd (1.3m)
Fabric 8	Peat	⅞yd (85cm)

Backing and Binding
Your choice of an Exotic Stripe from Fabrics 1-6

Backing	3⅜yd (3.2m)
Binding	⅝yd (60cm)

Batting
76in x 60in (194cm x 153cm)

PATCHES
Patches are half-square triangles (HSTs) cut in two different ways. In order to position stripes on the diagonal, all the striped fabrics are made from squares cut on point (with opposite corners positioned on a straight grain). This method produces triangles with a straight grain on the long side.
The shot cotton HSTs making up the other half of each square 'flag' are cut from squares cut across the width of the fabric. This method produces triangles with a straight grain on the short sides. Combining both methods stabilises the fabric and prevents stretching in bias seams. The finished HST squares are 5⅝in (14.3cm), and are set on point with inset border triangles and a 2in (5cm) finished border.

CUTTING OUT
Fabric is cut across the width unless otherwise stated. For best results, use spray starch before cutting.

Stripe Triangles
From each of **Fabrics 1-6** cut 8 squares 6½in (16.5cm) on point (with opposite corners positioned on a straight grain going down the stripes). Cross cut each square once diagonally **down the stripe** to create 2 HSTs, 16 from each fabric: 96 in total. You will use 90 of these.

Shot Cotton Triangles
From **Fabric 7** cut 7 strips 6½in (16.5cm) wide and cross cut squares at 6½in (16.5cm). Each strip will yield 6 squares giving you 42 squares in total. Cut each square once diagonally to create 84 HSTs, of which 83 are needed.

Inset Triangles and Border
From **Fabric 8** cut 2 strips 6½in (16.5cm) wide and cross cut 9 squares at 6½in (16.5cm). Cut 6 from the first strip and 3 from the second strip. Cut each square once diagonally to create 18 HSTs, of which 17 are needed.
Trim the remaining half strip to 4⅞in (12.4cm) wide and cross cut 2 squares at 4⅞in (12.4cm). Cross cut both squares once diagonally to create 4 HSTs, one for each corner.
From the remaining **Fabric 8** cut 6 strips 2½in (6.4cm) wide. Remove selvedges, sew end to end with ¼in (6mm) seams, and press seams open. From the length cut:
2 pieces 64½in (163.8cm) long for the side borders;
2 pieces 52½in (133.4cm) long for the top and bottom borders.

Backing
From your chosen Fabric 1-6 backing, cut 2 pieces 60in (152.4cm) wide. Remove selvedges and sew together along the length, then trim one end to make a backing piece 76in x 60in (194cm x 153cm).

FABRIC SWATCH DIAGRAM

Patchwork Fabrics

Fabric 1
EXOTIC STRIPE
Denim
WS04DM

Fabric 2
EXOTIC STRIPE
Desert
WS04DT

Fabric 3
EXOTIC STRIPE
Khaki
WS04KH

Fabric 4
EXOTIC STRIPE
Midnight
WS04MD

Fabric 5
EXOTIC STRIPE
Teal
WS04TE

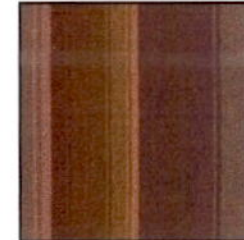
Fabric 6
EXOTIC STRIPE
Warm
WS04WM

Fabric 7
SHOT COTTON
Khaki
SC107KH

Fabric 8
SHOT COTTON
Peat
SC140PZ

Binding

Also from your chosen Fabric 1-6 backing and binding fabric, cut 7 strips 2½in (6.4cm) wide. Remove selvedges and sew end to end with 45° seams (see page 149).

MAKING THE QUILT

Using a design wall will help to place patches in the required layout.
Use ¼in (6mm) seams throughout.

Centre

Sew together 84 striped HSTs to 84 Fabric 7 HSTs down their long sides. Press lightly towards the stripy HSTs taking care not to stretch the fabric.
Referring to the Quilt Assembly Diagram and the quilt photograph, lay out the blocks on point in rows with the striped sides all to the right. Inset the left edge with the remaining striped triangles and inset the other three edges with Fabric 8 triangles. Add a Fabric 8 corner triangle to each corner.
Referring to the Quilt Assembly Diagram, sew the blocks together in diagonal rows, lightly pressing seams in opposite directions on alternate rows – odd rows to the left, even rows to the right – to allow the finished seams to lie flat. Sew the rows together taking care to align crossing seams.

Border

Pin (to prevent stretching) and sew the longer side borders to the centre, press seams towards the border, then pin and sew the top and bottom borders to the centre to complete the quilt top.

FINISHING THE QUILT

Press the quilt top. Layer the quilt top, batting and backing, and baste together (see page 148).
Quilt as desired.
Trim the quilt edges and attach the binding (see page 149).

QUILT ASSEMBLY DIAGRAM

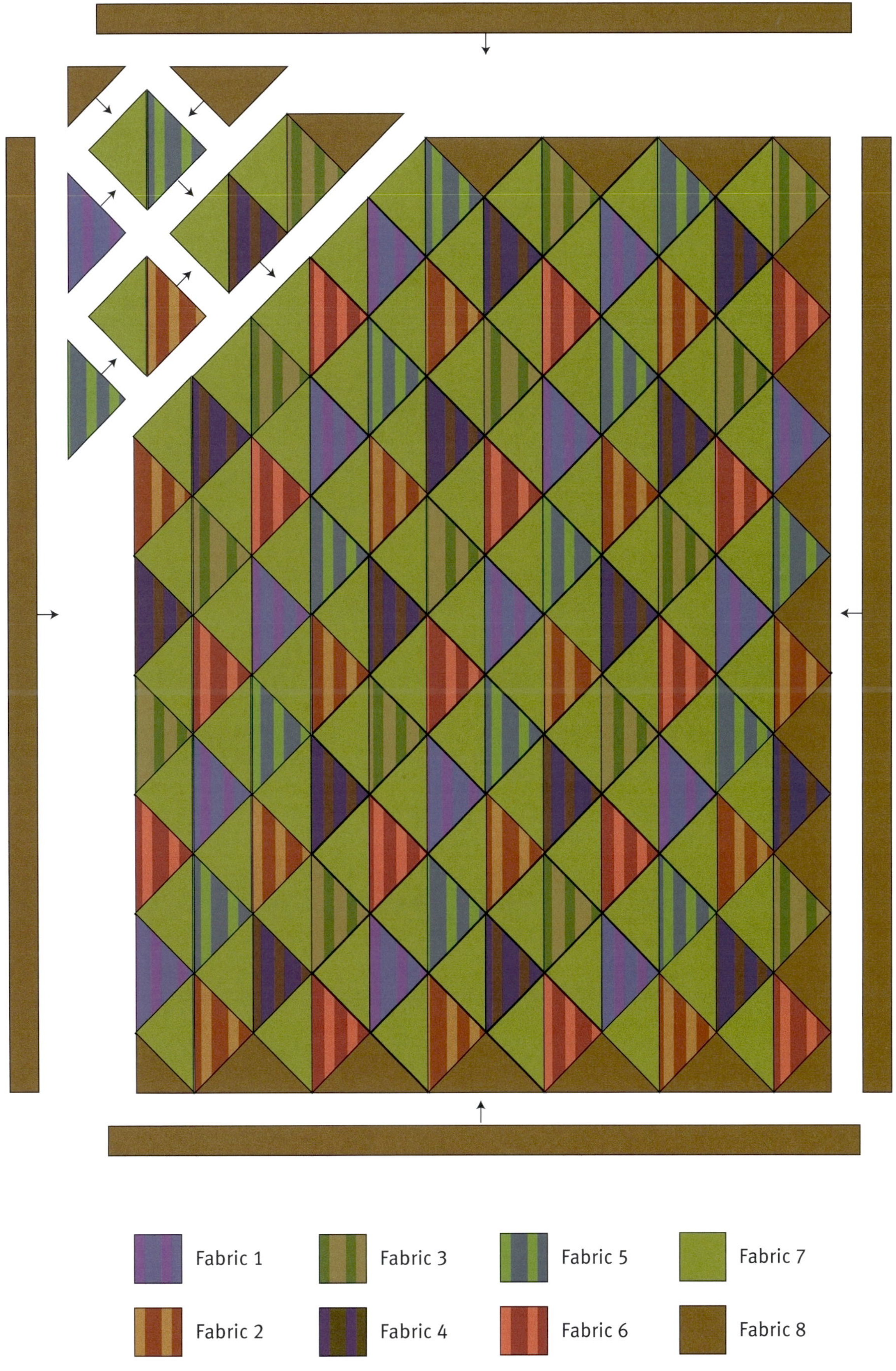

triangles and stripes cushions *

Kaffe Fassett

Rusty Exotic Stripe Cushion

Cool Wide Stripe Cushion

These two small cushions demonstrate different ways to use striped fabrics but employ similar construction methods.

SIZE OF FINISHED CUSHIONS

15in x 15in (38cm x 38cm)

FABRICS

Fabrics have been calculated at a maximum width of 40in (102cm). Fabrics have been given a number – see the Fabric Swatch Diagram for details.

Both cushions have a central square finished at 11in (27.9cm), created from 4 isosceles triangles either cut across or down the stripe. Each cushion is completed with a 2in (5.1cm) border and a backing with an envelope opening. For best results, use spray starch before cutting.

Patchwork Fabrics

Rusty Exotic Stripe Cushion

EXOTIC STRIPE

Fabric 1 Warm ⅜yd (40cm)

CATERPILLAR STRIPE

Fabric 2 Earth ¼yd (25cm)

WOBBLE

Fabric 3 Brown ⅜yd (40cm)

Cool Wide Stripe Cushion

BROAD STRIPE

Fabric 1 Azure ¼yd (25cm)

WOBBLE

Fabric 2 Blue ¼yd (25cm)

BLOOMERS

Fabric 3 Cobalt ⅜yd (40cm)

CUTTING OUT

Centre Triangles for Rusty Exotic Stripe

The long edge of the triangles will run **down** the stripes. From **Fabric 1** cut a strip 12¼in (31.1cm) wide. Cross cut 4 rectangles 6⅛in (15.6cm) wide. If you choose to match up the stripes to form a more uniform square, select similar positions across the stripes to cut your rectangles. There is enough fabric across the width to cut 4 very similar triangles. For a slightly skewed appearance, like the cushion shown, vary the position slightly from cut to cut. Mark the centre point of the inner side of each triangle and use the 45° line on your ruler to cut each short triangle edge.

Centre Triangles for Cool Wide Stripe
The long edge of the triangles will run **across** the stripes. From **Fabric 1** cut a strip 6⅛in (15.6cm) wide. Use the 45° line on your ruler to cross cut one short side of a triangle, then rotate the ruler, align the 45° line again and cross cut the second short side of the triangle. This cut also forms the first side of the second triangle. Continue across the strip and cut 4 triangles. There is enough fabric across the width to spread out the triangles a little if you wish to match up stripes more formally.

Border
From **Fabric 2** cut 2 strips across the width 2½in (6.4cm) wide. Cut 2 border pieces 11½in x 2½in (27.9cm x 6.4cm) and 2 border pieces 15½in x 2½in (39.4cm x 6.4cm).

Envelope Backing
From **Fabric 3** cut a strip across the width 10½in (26.7cm) wide and cross cut 2 rectangles 15½in x 10½in (39.4cm x 26.7cm).

CUSHION ASSEMBLY
Position the four triangles in your chosen layout, whether random or with similar opposite triangles. Referring to the Assembly Diagram and the photograph, sew 2 triangles together, then sew the other 2 triangles together, press seams in the same direction, then sew the two halves together.
Sew a **Fabric 2** short border piece to opposite sides of the square, then sew a long border piece to the remaining 2 sides.
Sew a narrow double hem on the side of each backing piece that will form the envelope opening. Place the 2 backing pieces with right sides facing the right side of the cushion top and with the hemmed edges overlapping across the middle of the cushion. Pin, then sew all the way around the cushion edge with a ¼in (6mm) seam, carefully snip the corners and turn the cushion the right way out, through the envelope opening.

FABRIC SWATCH DIAGRAM

Rusty Exotic Stripe Cushion

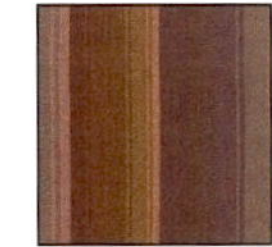
Fabric 1
EXOTIC STRIPE
Warm
WS04WM

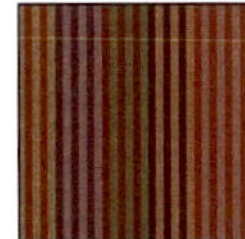
Fabric 2
CATERPILLAR STRIPE
Earth
WS01ER

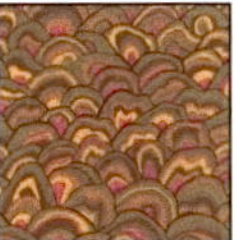
Fabric 3
WOBBLE
Brown
BM92BR

Cool Wide Stripe Cushion

Fabric 1
BROAD STRIPE
Azure
WS03AZ

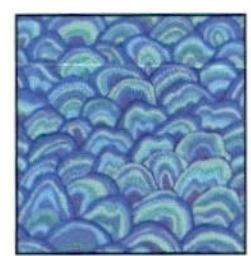
Fabric 2
WOBBLE
Blue
BM92BL

Fabric 3
BLOOMERS
Cobalt
BM93CB

ASSEMBLY DIAGRAM

Fabric 1

Fabric 2

templates

Refer to the individual quilt instructions for the templates needed. Look for the quilt name on the templates to make sure you are using the correct shapes for the project. Arrows on templates should be lined up with the straight grain of the fabric, which runs either along the selvedge or at 90 degrees to the selvedge. Following marked grain lines is important to avoid bias edges, which can cause distortion.

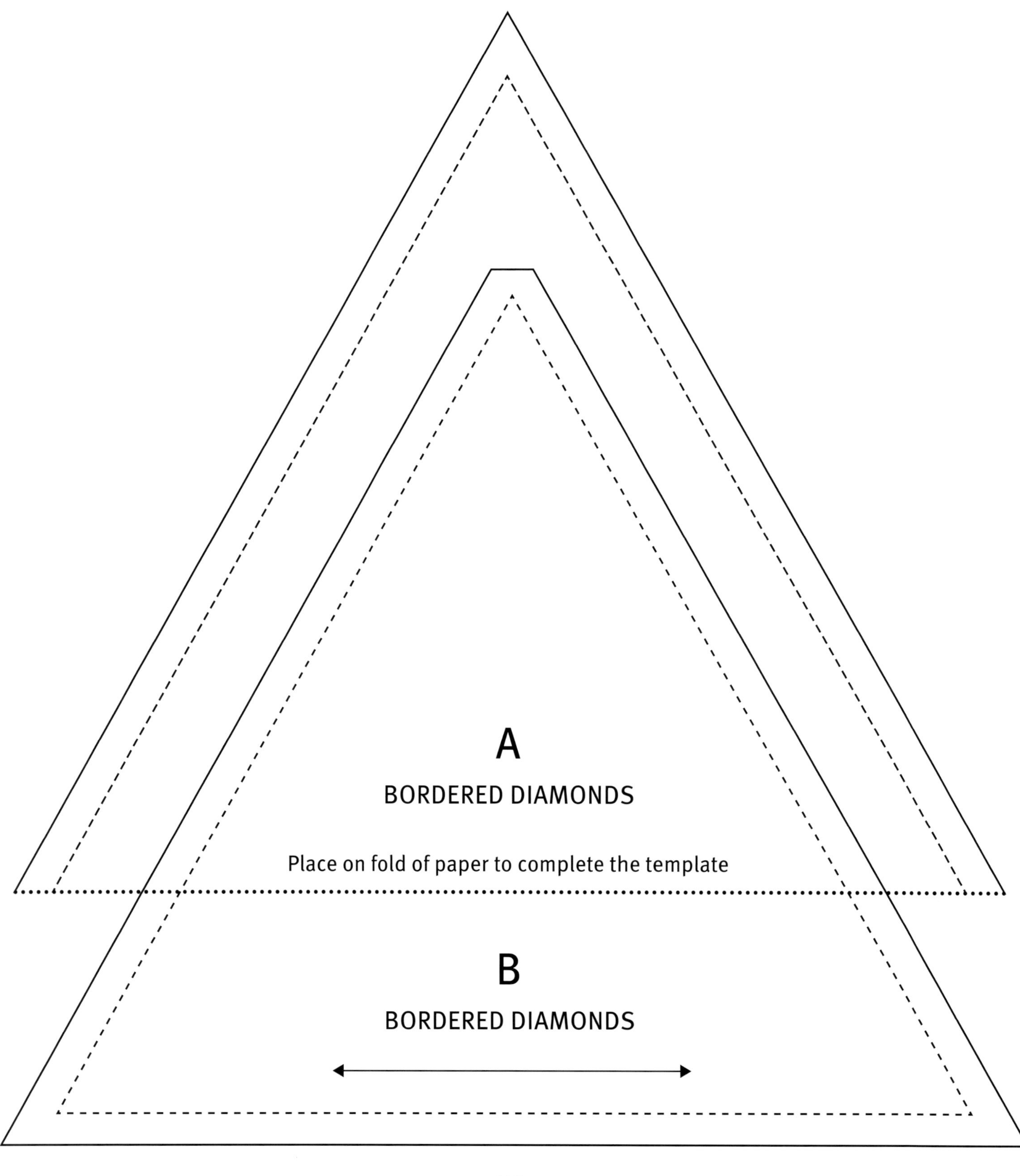

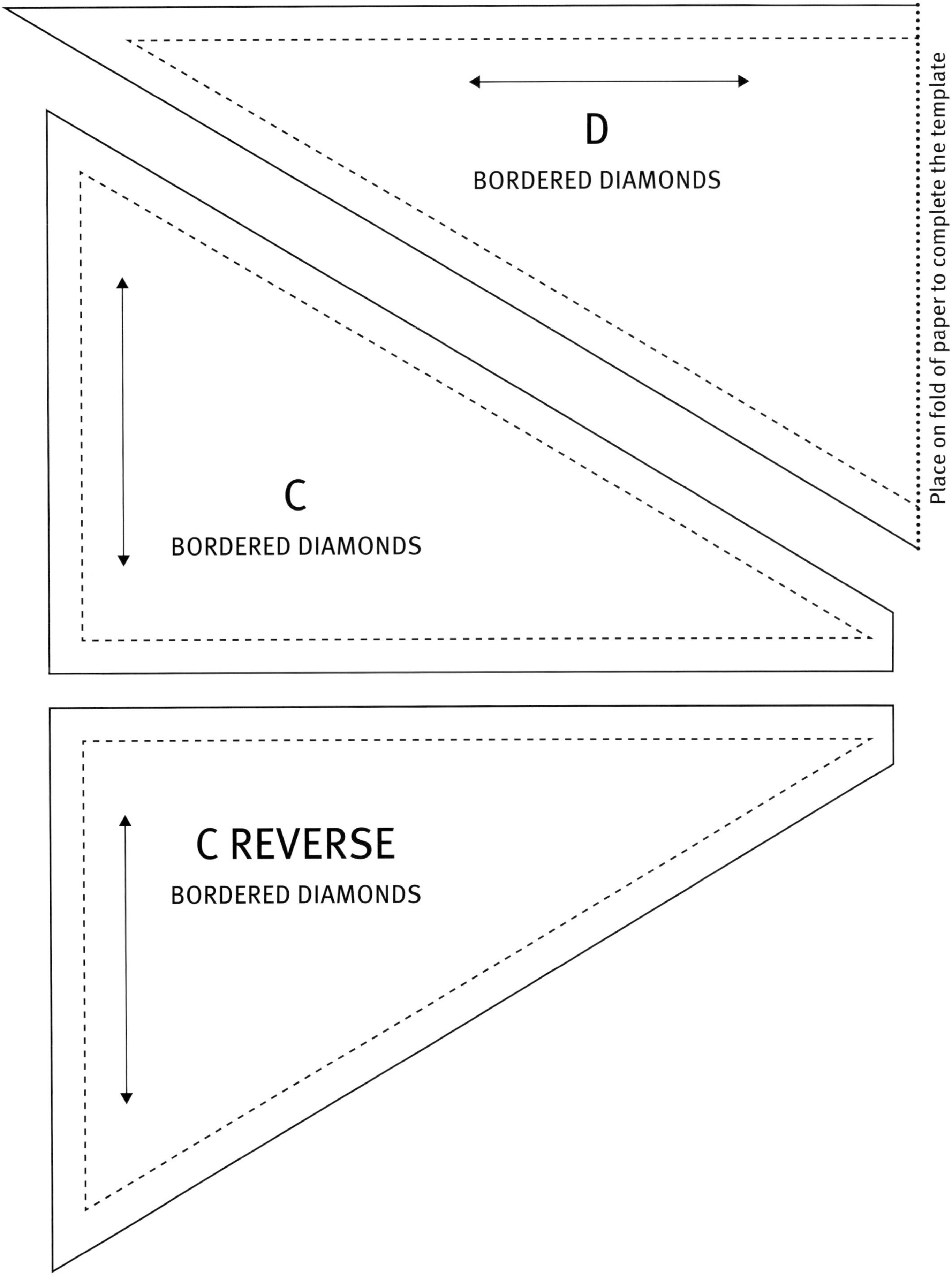

D

BORDERED DIAMONDS

Place on fold of paper to complete the template

C

BORDERED DIAMONDS

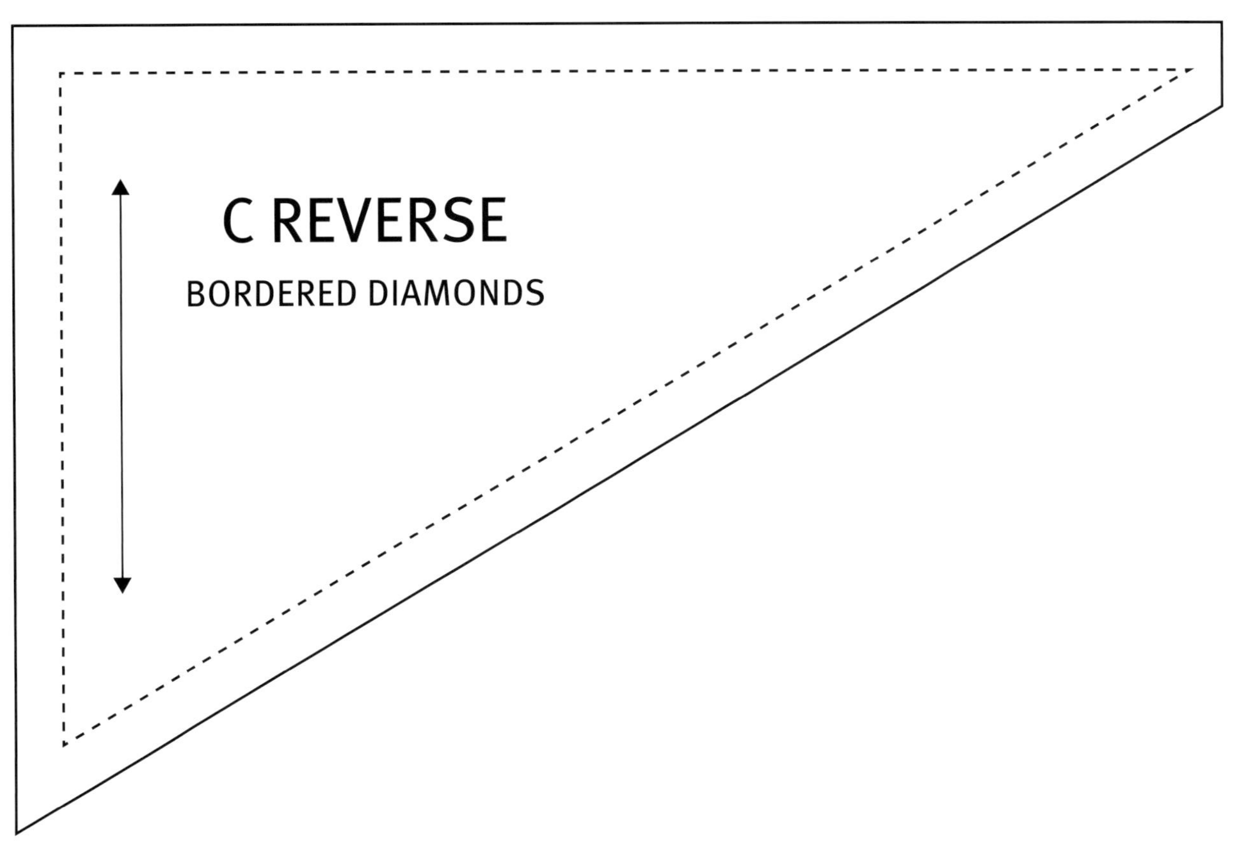

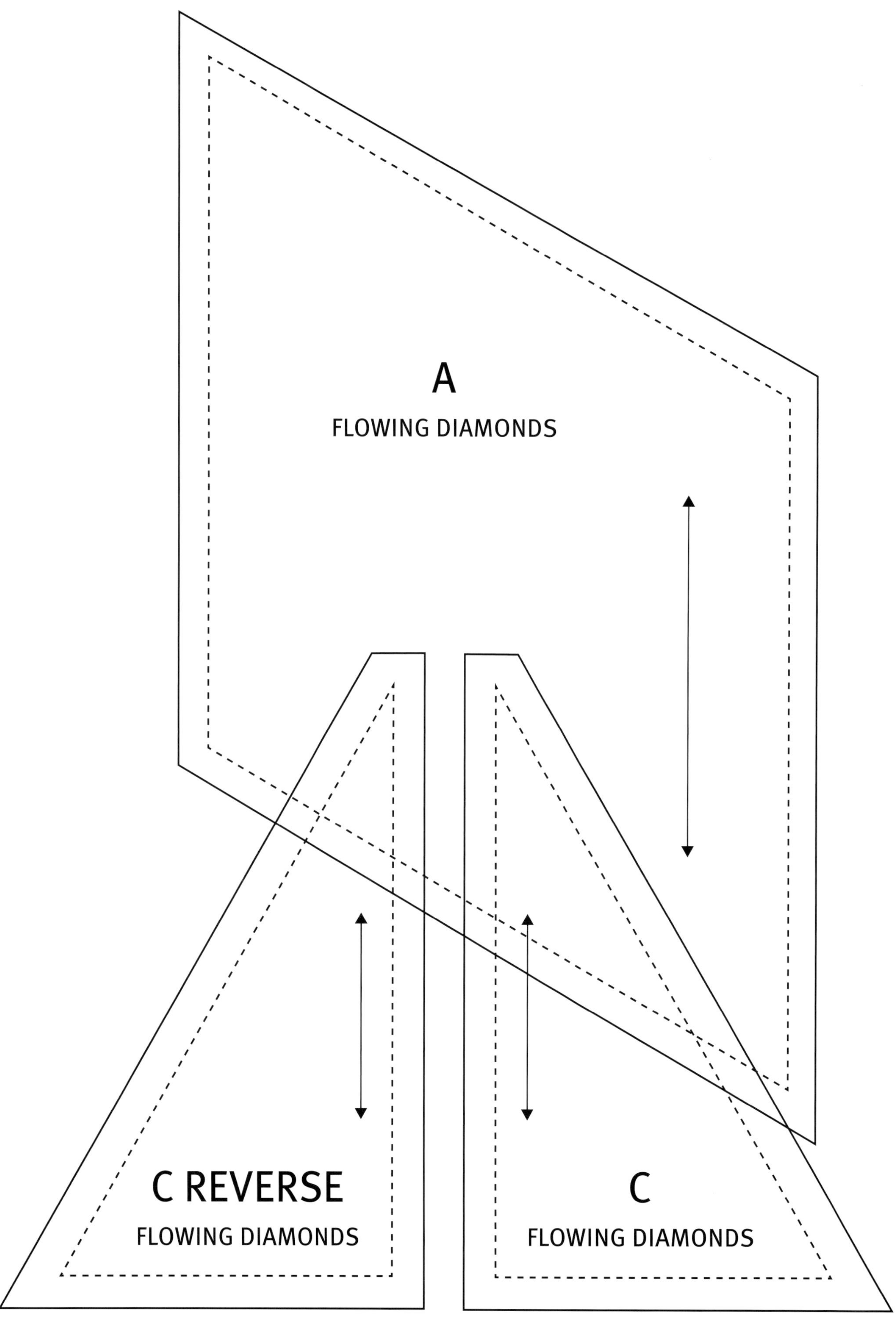
A
FLOWING DIAMONDS
C REVERSE
FLOWING DIAMONDS
C
FLOWING DIAMONDS

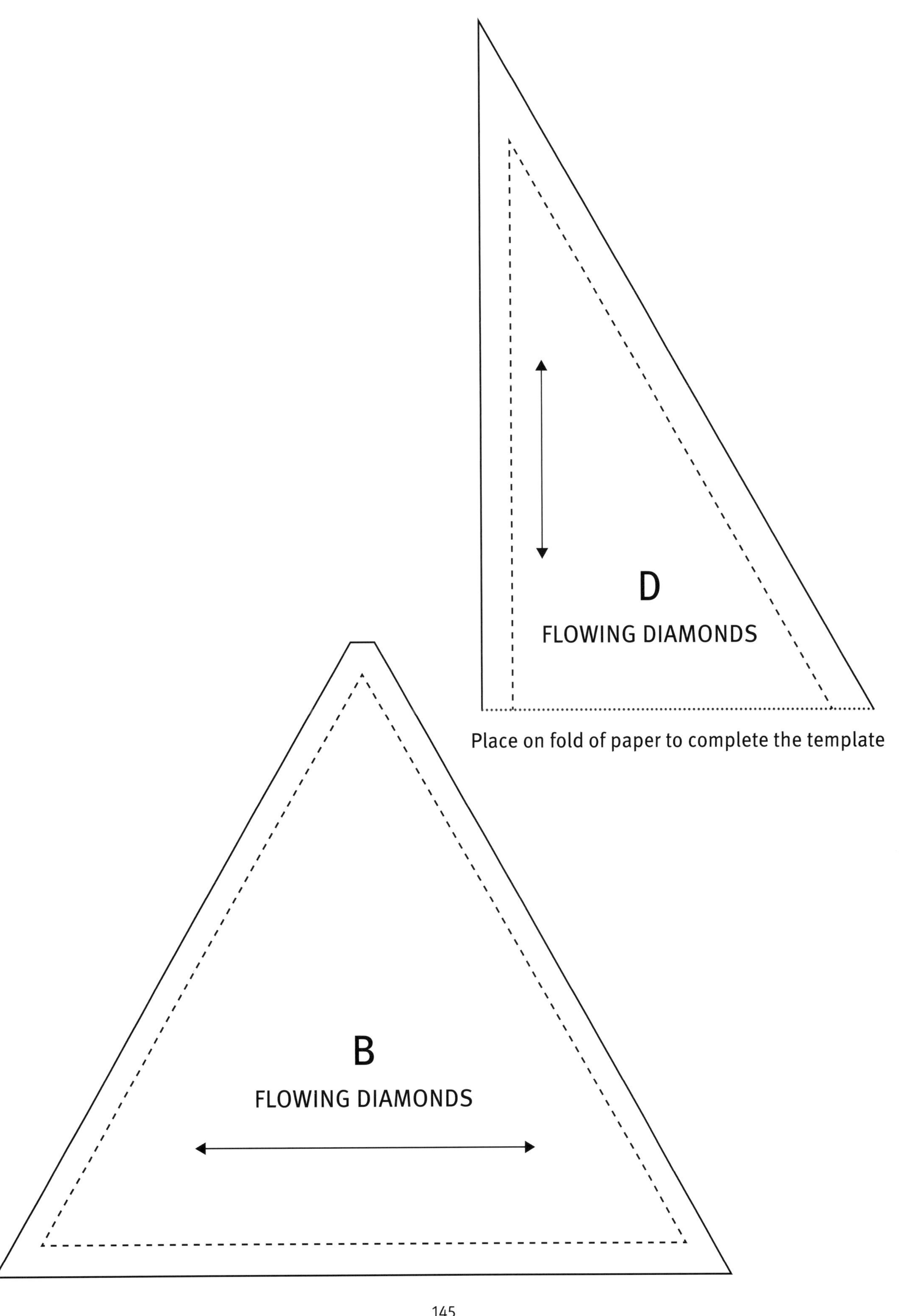
D
FLOWING DIAMONDS
Place on fold of paper to complete the template
B
FLOWING DIAMONDS

patchwork and quilting know-how

These instructions are intended for the novice quilt maker, providing the basic information needed to make the projects in this book, along with some useful tips.

EXPERIENCE RATINGS

* Easy, straightforward, suitable for a beginner.
** Suitable for the average patchworker and quilter.
*** For the more experienced patchworker and quilter.

ABOUT THE FABRICS

The fabrics used for the quilts in this book are mainly from Kaffe Fassett Collective:
GP is the code for Kaffe Fassett's designs, **PJ** for Philip Jacobs' and **BM** for Brandon Mably's.
The other fabrics used are Shot Cottons and Stripes with SC or SS prefixes as well as wide backing fabrics with QB prefixes.

PREPARING THE FABRIC

Prewash all new fabrics before you begin, to ensure that there will be no uneven shrinkage and no bleeding of colours when the finished quilt is laundered. Press the fabric whilst it is still damp to return crispness to it. All fabric requirements in this book are calculated on a 40in (102cm) usable fabric width, to allow for shrinkage and selvedge removal.

MAKING TEMPLATES

Transparent template plastic is the best material to use: it is durable and allows you to see the fabric and select certain motifs. You can also use tracing paper and thin stiff cardboard.

Templates for machine piecing

1 Trace off the actual-sized template provided either directly on to template plastic, or on to tracing paper and then on to thin cardboard. Use a ruler to help you trace off the straight cutting line, dotted seam line and grain lines.

Sometimes templates are too large to print complete. Transfer the template on to the fold of a large sheet of paper, cut out and open out for the full template. Some templates are printed at a reduced size and need to be scaled up on a photocopier.

2 Cut out the traced off template using a craft knife, a ruler and a self-healing cutting mat.

3 Punch holes in the corners of the template, at each point on the seam line, using a hole punch.

Templates for hand piecing

• Make a template as for machine piecing, but do not trace off the cutting line. Use the dotted seam line as the outer edge of the template.

• This template allows you to draw the seam lines directly on to the fabric. The seam allowances can then be cut by eye around the patch.

CUTTING THE FABRIC

On the individual instructions for each project, you will find a summary of all the patch shapes used.

Always mark and cut out any border and binding strips first, followed by the largest patch shapes and finally the smallest ones, to make the most efficient use of your fabric. The border and binding strips are best cut using a rotary cutter.

Rotary cutting

Rotary cut strips are usually cut across the fabric from selvedge to selvedge, but some projects may vary, so please read through all the instructions before you start cutting the fabrics.

1 Before beginning to cut, press out any folds or creases in the fabric. If you are cutting a large piece of fabric, you will need to fold it several times to fit the cutting mat. When there is only a single fold, place the fold facing you. If the fabric is too wide to be folded only once, fold it concertina-style until it fits your mat. A small rotary cutter with a sharp blade will cut up to six layers of fabric; a large cutter up to eight layers.

2 To ensure that your cut strips are straight and even, the folds must be placed exactly parallel to the straight edges of the fabric and along a line on the cutting mat.

3 Place a rotary ruler over the raw edge of the fabric, overlapping it about ½in (1.25cm). Make sure that the ruler is at right angles to both the straight edges and the fold to ensure that you cut along the straight grain. Press down on the ruler and wheel the cutter away from you along the edge of the ruler.

4 Open out the fabric to check the edge. Don't worry if it's not perfectly straight – a little wiggle will not show when the quilt is stitched together. Re-fold the fabric, then place the ruler over the trimmed edge, aligning the edge with the markings on the ruler that match the correct strip width. Cut strip along the edge of the ruler.

USING TEMPLATES

The most efficient way to cut out templates is by first rotary cutting a strip of fabric to the width stated for your template, and then marking off your templates along the strip, edge to edge at the required angle. This method leaves hardly any waste and gives a random effect to your patches.

A less efficient method is to fussy cut them, where the templates are cut individually by placing them on particular motifs or stripes, to create special effects. Although this method is more wasteful, it yields very interesting results.

1 Place the template face down, on the wrong side of the fabric, with the grain-line arrow following the straight grain of the fabric, if indicated. Be careful though – check with your individual instructions, as some instructions may ask you to cut patches on varying grains.

2 Hold the template firmly in place and draw around it with a sharp pencil or crayon, marking in the corner dots or seam lines. To save fabric, position patches close together or even touching. Don't worry if outlines positioned on the straight grain when drawn on striped fabrics do not always match the stripes when cut – this will add a degree of visual excitement to the patchwork!

3 Once you've drawn all the pieces needed, you are ready to cut the fabric, with either a rotary cutter and ruler or a pair of sharp sewing scissors.

Basic hand and machine piecing

Patches can be stitched together by hand or machine. Machine stitching is quicker, but hand assembly allows you to carry your patches around with you and work on them in every spare moment. The choice is yours. For techniques that are new to you, practise on scrap pieces of fabric until you feel confident.

Hand piecing
1 Pin two patches with right sides together, so that the marked seam lines are facing outwards.

2 Using a single strand of strong thread, secure the corner of a seam line with a couple of back stitches.

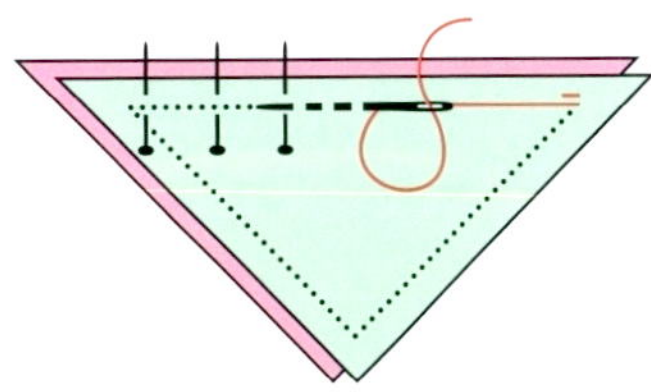

3 Sew running stitches along the marked line, working 8–10 stitches per inch (2.5cm) and ending at the opposite seam line corner with a few back stitches. When hand piecing never stitch over the seam allowances.

4 Press the seams to one side, as shown in machine piecing (Step 2).

Machine piecing
Follow the quilt instructions for the order in which to piece the individual patchwork blocks and then assemble the blocks together in rows.

1 Seam lines are not marked on the fabric for simple shapes, so stitch ¼in (6mm) seams using the machine needle plate, a ¼in (6mm) wide machine foot, or tape stuck to the machine as a guide. Pin two patches with right sides together, matching edges.

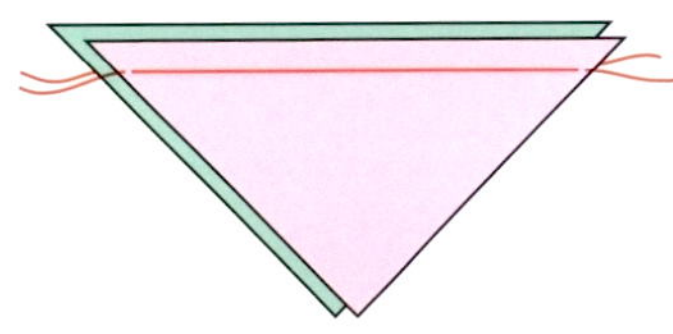

For some shapes, particularly diamonds, you need to match the sewing lines, not the fabric edges. Place 2 diamonds right sides together but offset so that the sewing lines intersect at the correct position. Use pins to secure for sewing.

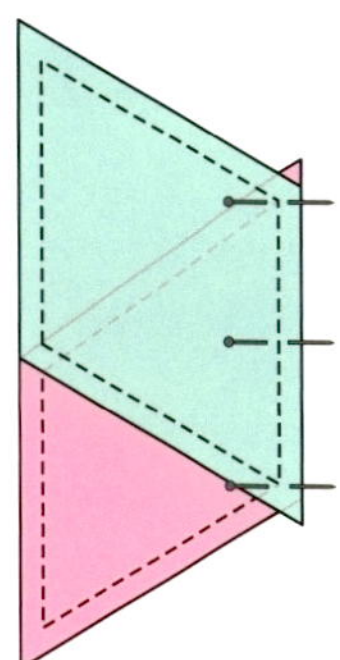

Set your machine at 10–12 stitches per inch (2.5cm) and stitch seams from edge to edge, removing pins as you feed the fabric through the machine.

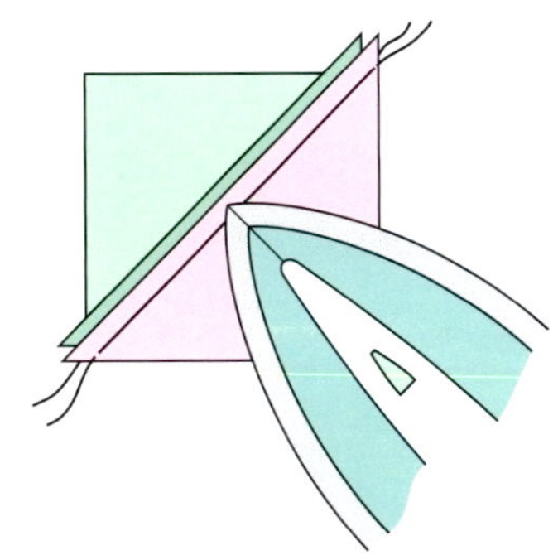

2 Press the seams of each patchwork block to one side before attempting to join it to another block. When joining diamond shaped blocks you will need to offset the blocks in the same way as diamond shaped patches, matching the sewing lines, not the fabric edges.

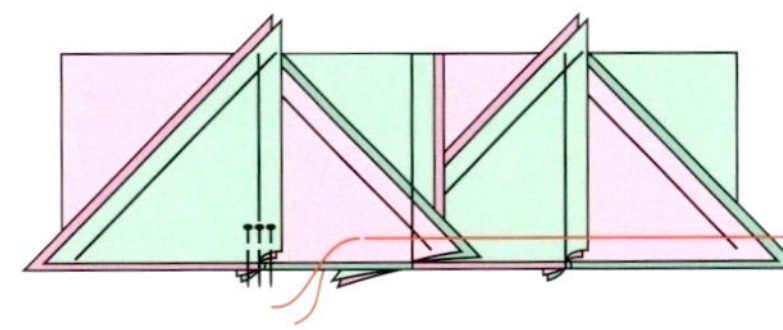

3 When joining rows of blocks, make sure that adjacent seam allowances are pressed in opposite directions to reduce bulk and make matching easier. Pin pieces together directly through the stitch line and to the right and left of the seam. Remove pins as you sew. Continue pressing seams to one side as you work.

Inset (Y) seams
When 3 or more patches have seams that come together without making a rectangle (i.e. in a Y-shape), an inset seam is needed. As shown in the diagram, with RS together, first sew the A–B seam. Then, starting from an inner point to an outer point, sew the A–C seam, and finally the A–D seam. Make sure you start and finish each ¼in (6mm) seam exactly at the beginning and end (as marked by dots on the diagram) and do not stitch into the seam allowance.

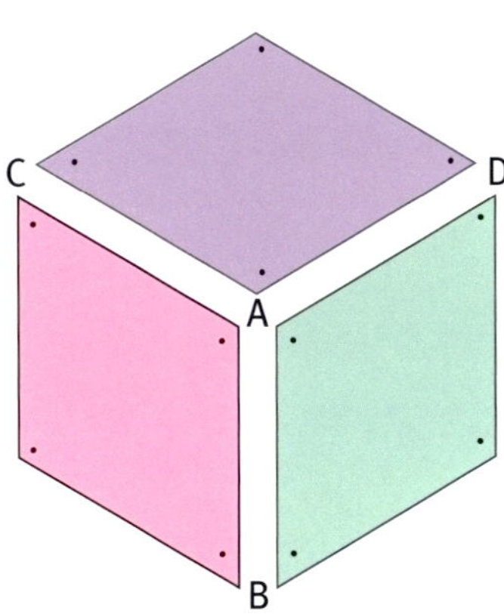

MACHINE APPLIQUÉ WITH ADHESIVE WEB
To make appliqué very easy you can use adhesive web (which comes attached to a paper backing sheet) to bond the motifs to the background fabric. There are two types of web available: the first keeps the pieces in place while they are stitched, the second permanently attaches the pieces so that no sewing is required. Follow steps 1 and 2 for the non-sew type and steps 1–3 for the type that requires sewing.

1 Trace the reversed appliqué design onto the paper side of the adhesive web, leaving a ¼in (6mm) gap between all the shapes. Roughly cut out the motifs ⅛in (3mm) outside your drawn line.

2 Bond the motifs to the reverse of your chosen fabrics. Cut out on the drawn line with very sharp scissors. Remove the backing paper by scoring the centre of the motif carefully with a scissor point and peeling the paper away from the centre out (to prevent damage to the edges). Place the motifs onto the background, noting any which may be layered. Cover with a clean cloth and bond with a hot iron (check instructions for temperature setting as adhesive web can vary depending on the manufacturer).

3 Using a contrasting or toning coloured thread in your machine, work small close zig zag stitches (or a blanket stitch if your machine has one) around the edge of the motifs; the majority of the stitching should sit on the appliqué shape. When stitching up to points, stop with the machine needle in the down position, lift the foot of your machine, pivot the work, lower the foot and continue to stitch. Make sure all the raw edges are stitched.

HAND APPLIQUÉ
Good preparation is essential for speedy and accurate hand appliqué. The finger-pressing method is suitable for needle-turning application, used for simple shapes like leaves and flowers. Using a card template is the best method for bold simple motifs such as circles.

Finger–pressing method
1 To make your template, transfer the appliqué design using carbon paper on to stiff card, and cut out the template. Trace around the outline of your appliquéd shape on to the right side of your fabric using a well sharpened pencil. Cut out shapes, adding by eye a ¼in (6mm) seam allowance all around.

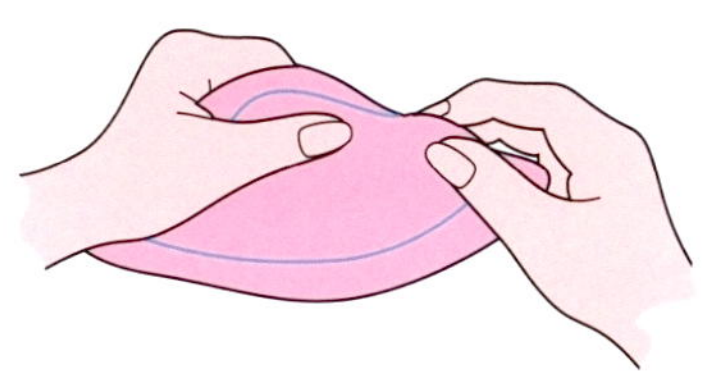

2 Hold the shape right side up and fold under the seam, turning along your drawn line, pinch to form a crease. Dampening the fabric makes this very easy. When using shapes with points such as leaves, turn in the seam allowance at the point first, as shown in the diagram. Then continue all round the shape. If your shapes have sharp curves, you can snip the seam allowance to ease the curve. Take care not to stretch the appliqué shapes as you work.

Straight stems

Place fabric face down and simply press over the ¼in (6mm) seam allowance along each edge. You don't need to finish the ends of stems that are layered under other appliqué shapes. Where the end of the stem is visible, simply tuck under the end and finish neatly.

Needle-turning application

Take the appliqué shape and pin in position. Stroke the seam allowance under with the tip of the needle as far as the creased pencil line, and hold securely in place with your thumb. Using a matching thread, bring the needle up from the back of the block into the edge of the shape and proceed to blind-hem in place. (This stitch allows the motifs to appear to be held on invisibly.) To do this, bring the thread out from below through the folded edge of the motif, never on the top. The stitches must be small, even and close together to prevent the seam allowance from unfolding and from frayed edges appearing. Try to avoid pulling the stitches too tight, as this will cause the motifs to pucker up. Work around the whole shape, stroking under each small section before sewing.

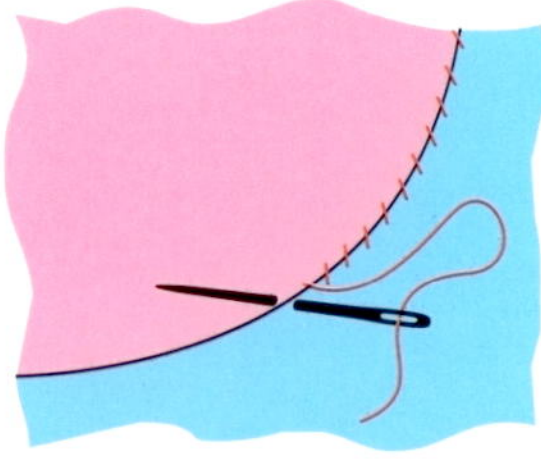

QUILTING

When you have finished piecing your patchwork and added any borders, press it carefully. It is now ready for quilting.

Marking quilting designs and motifs

Many tools are available for marking quilting patterns, check the manufacturer's instructions for use and test on scraps of fabric from your project. Use an acrylic ruler for marking straight lines.

Stencils

Some designs require stencils; these can be made at home, by transferring the designs on to template plastic, or stiff cardboard. The design is then cut away in the form of long dashes, to act as guides for both internal and external lines. These stencils are a quick method for producing an identical set of repeated designs.

BACKING FABRIC

The quilts in this book use two different widths of backing fabric – the standard width of 44in (112cm) and a wider one of 108in (274cm). If you can't find (or don't want to use) the wider fabric then select a standard-width fabric instead and adjust the amount accordingly. For most of the quilts in the book, using a standard-width fabric will probably mean joins in the fabric. The material list for each quilt assumes that an extra 4in of backing fabric is needed all round (8in in total) when making up the quilt sandwich, to allow for long-arm quilting if needed. We have assumed a usable width of 40in (102cm), to allow for selvedge removal and possible shrinkage after washing.

Preparing the backing and batting

- Remove the selvedges and piece together the backing fabric to form a backing at least 4in (10cm) larger all around than the patchwork top.

- Choose a fairly thin batting, preferably pure cotton, to give your quilt a flat appearance. If your batting has been rolled up, unroll it and let it rest before cutting it to the same size as the backing.

- For a large quilt it may be necessary to join two pieces of batting to fit. Lay the pieces of batting on a flat surface so that they overlap by around 8in (20cm). Cut a curved line through both layers.

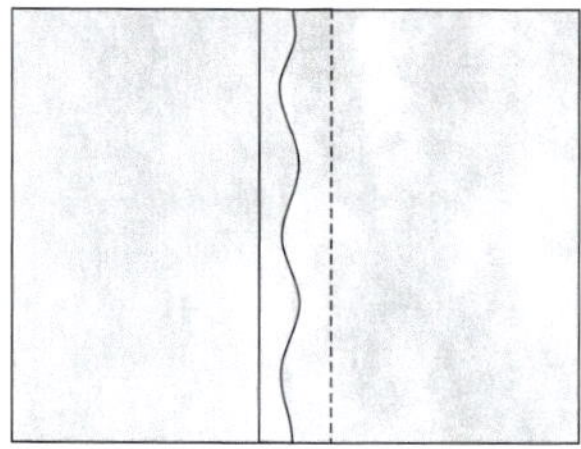

- Carefully peel away the two narrow pieces and discard. Butt the curved cut edges back together. Stitch the two pieces together using a large herringbone stitch.

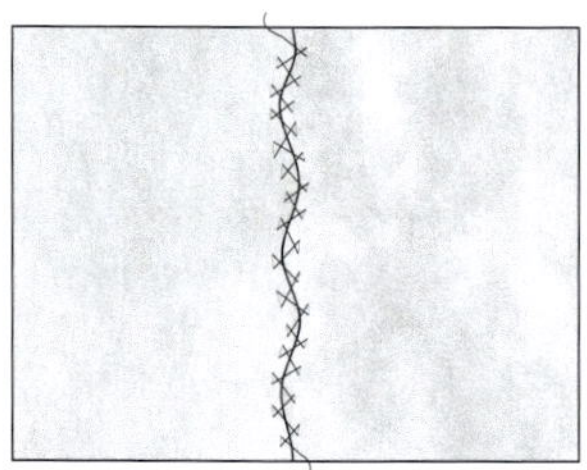

BASTING THE LAYERS TOGETHER

1 On the floor or on a large work surface, lay out the backing with wrong side uppermost. Use weights along the edges to keep it taut.

2 Lay the batting on the backing and smooth it out gently. Next lay the patchwork top, right side up, on top of the batting and smooth gently until there are no wrinkles. Pin at the corners and at the midpoints of each side, close to the edges.

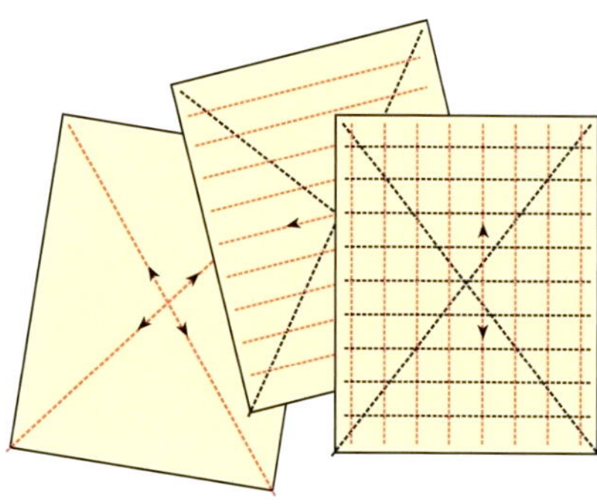

3 Beginning at the centre, baste diagonal lines outwards to the corners, making your stitches about 3in (7.5cm) long. Then, again starting at the centre, baste horizontal and vertical lines out to the edges. Continue basting until you have basted a grid of lines about 4in (10cm) apart over the entire quilt.

4 For speed, when machine quilting, some quilters prefer to baste their quilt sandwich layers together using rust-proof safety pins, spaced at 4in (10cm) intervals over the entire quilt.

HAND QUILTING

This is best done with the quilt mounted on a quilting frame or hoop, but as long as you have basted the quilt well, a frame is not essential. With the quilt top facing upwards, begin at the centre of the quilt and make even running stitches following the design. It is more important to make even stitches on both sides of the quilt than to make small ones. Start and finish your stitching with back stitches and bury the ends of your threads in the batting.

TIED QUILTING

If you prefer you could use tied quilting rather than machine quilting. For tied quilting, use a strong thread that will withstand being pulled through the quilt layers and tied in a knot. You can tie with the knot on the front of the quilt or the back, as preferred. Leaving tufts of thread gives an attractive, rustic look.

Thread a needle with a suitable thread, using the number of strands noted in the project. Put the needle and thread through from the front of the work, leaving a long tail. Go through to the back of the quilt, make a small stitch and then come back through to the front. Tie the threads together using a reef knot and trim the thread ends to the desired length. For extra security, you could tie a double knot or add a spot of fabric glue on the knot.

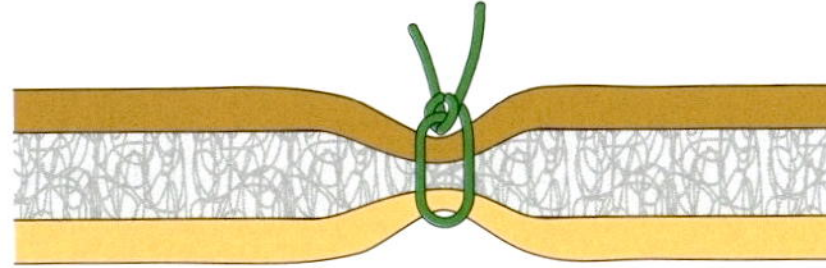

MACHINE QUILTING

- For a flat looking quilt, always use a walking foot on your machine for stitching straight lines, and a darning foot for free-motion quilting.

- It is best to start your quilting at the centre of the quilt and work out towards the borders, doing the straight quilting lines first (stitch-in-the-ditch) followed by the free-motion quilting.

- When free-motion quilting, stitch in a loose meandering style as shown in the diagrams. Do not stitch too closely as this will make the quilt feel stiff when finished. If you wish you can include floral themes or follow shapes on the printed fabrics for added interest.

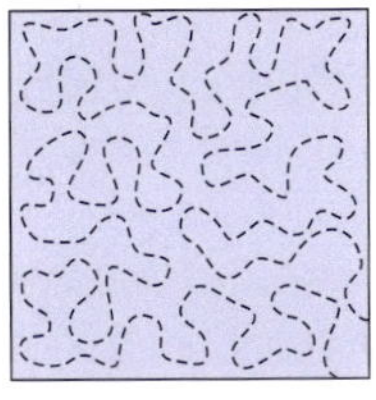

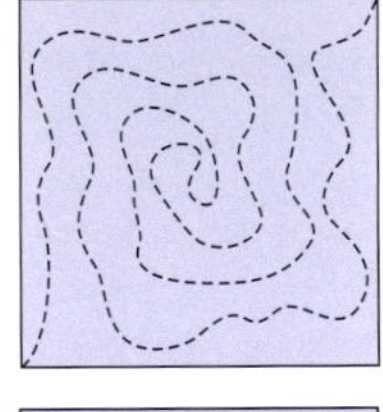

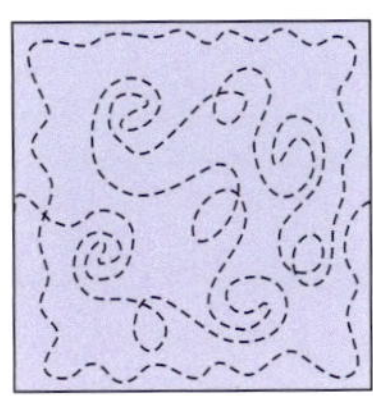

- Make it easier for yourself by handling the quilt properly. Roll up the excess quilt neatly to fit under your sewing machine arm, and use a table or chair to help support the weight of the quilt that hangs down the other side.

FINISHING

Preparing to bind the edges

Once you have quilted or tied your quilt sandwich together, remove all the basting stitches. Then, baste around the outer edge of the quilt ¼in (6mm) from the edge of the top patchwork layer. Trim the back and batting to the edge of the patchwork and straighten the edge of the patchwork if necessary.

Binding and 45-degree seams

1 Cut bias or straight grain strips the width required for your binding, making sure the grain-line is running the correct way on your straight grain strips. Cut enough strips until you have the required length to go around the edge of your quilt.

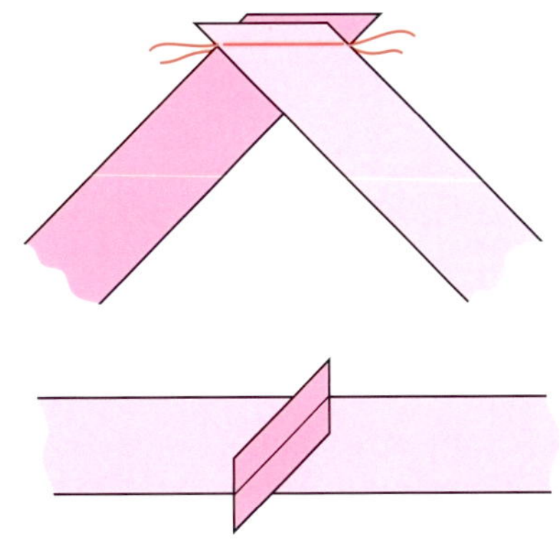

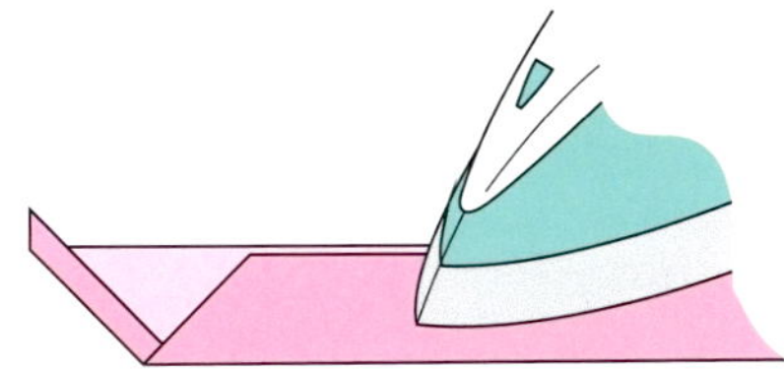

2 To join strips together, the two ends that are to be joined must be cut at a 45-degree angle, as above. Stitch right sides together, trim turnings and press seam open.

Binding the edges

1 Cut the starting end of binding strip at a 45-degree angle, fold a ¼in (6mm) turning to wrong side along cut edge and press in place. With wrong sides together, fold strip in half lengthways, keeping raw edges level, and press.

2 Starting at the centre of one of the long edges, place the doubled binding on to the right side of the quilt keeping raw edges level. Stitch the binding in place. starting ¼in (6mm) in from the diagonal folded edge. Reverse stitch to secure, and work ¼in (6mm) in from edge of the quilt towards first corner of quilt. Stop ¼in (6mm) in from corner and work a few reverse stitches.

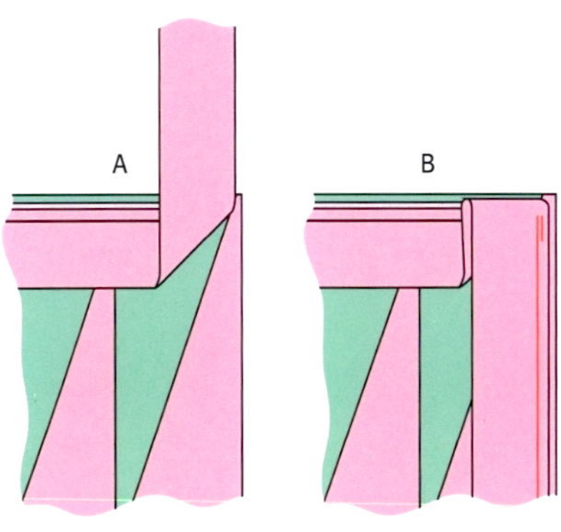

3 Fold the loose end of the binding up, making a 45-degree angle (see A). Keeping the diagonal fold in place, fold the binding back down, aligning the raw edges with the next side of the quilt. Starting at the point where the last stitch ended, stitch down the next side (see B).

4 Continue to stitch the binding in place around all the quilt edges in this way, tucking the finishing end of the binding inside the diagonal starting section.

5 Turn the folded edge of the binding on to the back of the quilt. Hand stitch the folded edge in place just covering binding machine stitches, and folding a mitre at each corner.

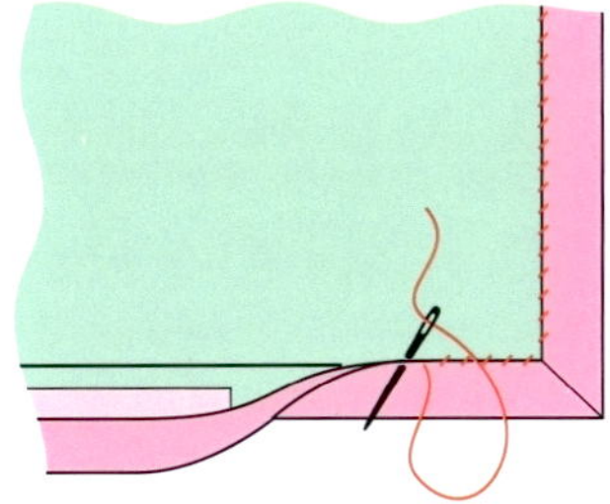

glossary of terms

Adhesive or fusible web This comes attached to a paper-backed sheet and is used to bond appliqué motifs to a background fabric. There are 2 types of web available, the first keeps the pieces in place whilst they are stitched, the second permanently attaches the pieces so that no sewing is required.

Appliqué The technique of stitching fabric shapes on to a background to create a design. It can be applied either by hand or machine with a decorative embroidery stitch, such as buttonhole, or satin stitch.

Backing The bottom layer of a quilt sandwich. It is made of fabric pieced to the size of the quilt top with the addition of about 4in (10cm) all around to allow for quilting take-up.

Basting or tacking This is a means of holding two fabric layers or the layers of a quilt sandwich together temporarily with large hand stitches or pins.

Batting or wadding This is the middle layer, or padding in a quilt. It can be made of cotton, wool, silk or synthetic fibres.

Bias The diagonal grain of a fabric. This is the direction which has the most give or stretch, making it ideal for bindings, especially on curved edges.

Binding A narrow strip of fabric used to finish off the edges of quilts or projects; it can be cut on the straight grain of a fabric or on the bias.

Block A single design unit that when stitched together with other blocks create the quilt top. It is most often a square, hexagon, or rectangle, but it can be any shape. It can be pieced or plain.

Border A frame of fabric stitched to the outer edges of the quilt top. Borders can be narrow or wide, pieced or plain. As well as making the quilt larger, they unify the overall design and draw attention to the central area.

Chalk pencils Available in various colours, they are used for marking lines or spots on fabric.

Cutting mat Designed for use with a rotary cutter, it is made from a special self-healing material that keeps your cutting blade sharp. Cutting mats come in various sizes and are usually marked with a grid to help you line up the edges of fabric and cut out larger pieces.

Design wall Used for laying out fabric patches before sewing. A large wall or folding board covered with flannel fabric or cotton batting in a neutral shade (dull beige or grey work well) will hold fabric in place so that an overall view can be taken of the placement.

Free-motion quilting Curved wavy quilting lines stitched in a random manner. Stitching diagrams are often given for you to follow as a loose guide.

Fussy cutting This is when a template is placed on a particular motif, or stripe, to obtain interesting effects. This method is not as efficient as strip cutting, but yields very interesting results.

Grain The direction in which the threads run in a woven fabric. In a vertical direction it is called the lengthwise grain, which has very little stretch. The horizontal direction, or crosswise grain is slightly stretchy, but diagonally the fabric has a lot of stretch. This grain is called the bias. Wherever possible the grain of a fabric should run in the same direction on a quilt block and borders.

Grain lines These are arrows printed on templates which should be aligned with the fabric grain.

Inset seams or setting-in A patchwork technique whereby one patch (or block) is stitched into a Y shape formed by the joining of two other patches (or blocks).

Patch A small shaped piece of fabric used in the making of a patchwork pattern.

Patchwork The technique of stitching small pieces of fabric (patches) together to create a larger piece of fabric, usually forming a design.

Pieced quilt A quilt composed of patches.

Quilting Traditionally done by hand with running stitches, but for speed modern quilts are often stitched by machine. The stitches are sewn through the top, wadding and backing to hold the three layers together. Quilting stitches are usually worked in some form of design, but they can be random.

Quilting hoop Consists of two wooden circular or oval rings with a screw adjuster on the outer ring. It stabilises the quilt layers, helping to create an even tension.

Reducing glass Used for viewing the complete composition of a quilt at a glance. It works like a magnifier in reverse. A useful tool for checking fabric placement before piecing a quilt.

Rotary cutter A sharp circular blade attached to a handle for quick, accurate cutting. It is a device that can be used to cut several layers of fabric at one time. It must be used in conjunction with a self-healing cutting mat and a thick plastic ruler.

Rotary ruler A thick, clear plastic ruler marked with lines in imperial or metric measurements. Sometimes they also have diagonal lines indicating 45 and 60 degree angles. A rotary ruler is used as a guide when cutting out fabric pieces using a rotary cutter.

Sashing A piece or pieced sections of fabric interspaced between blocks.

Sashing posts When blocks have sashing between them the corner squares are known as sashing posts.

Selvedges Also known as selvages, these are the firmly woven edges down each side of a fabric length. Selvedges should be trimmed off before cutting out your fabric, as they are more liable to shrink when the fabric is washed.

Stitch-in-the-ditch or Ditch quilting Also known as quilting-in-the-ditch. The quilting stitches are worked along the actual seam lines to give a pieced quilt texture.

Template A pattern piece used as a guide for marking and cutting out fabric patches, or marking a quilting, or appliqué design. Usually made from plastic or strong card that can be reused many times. Templates for cutting fabric usually have marked grain lines which should be aligned with the fabric grain.

Threads One hundred percent cotton or cotton-covered polyester is best for hand and machine piecing. Choose a colour that matches your fabric. When sewing different colours and patterns together, choose a medium to light neutral colour, such as grey or ecru. Specialist quilting threads are available for hand and machine quilting.

Walking foot or Quilting foot This is a sewing machine foot with dual feed control. It is very helpful when quilting, as the fabric layers are fed evenly from the top and below, reducing the risk of slippage and puckering.

Yo-Yos A circle of fabric double the size of the finished puff is gathered up into a rosette shape.

Y seams See Inset seams.

OTHER TAUNTON TITLES AVAILABLE

Kaffe Fassett's Quilts en Provence
Kaffe Fassett's Quilts in Sweden
Kaffe Quilts Again
Kaffe Fassett's Quilt Grandeur
Kaffe Fassett's Quilts in Morocco
Kaffe Fassett's Heritage Quilts
Kaffe Fassett's Quilts in Italy
Kaffe Fassett's Quilts in Ireland
Kaffe Fassett's Quilts in America
Kaffe Fassett's Quilts in the Cotswolds
Kaffe Fassett's Quilts in Burano
Kaffe Fassett's Quilts in an English Village
Kaffe Fassett's Quilts in Wales
Kaffe Fassett's Quilts by the Sea
Kaffe Fassett's Quilts on an English Farm

To find a retailer in your part of the world for fabrics used in this book, please go to www.freespiritfabrics.com/where-to-buy/

The fabric collection can be viewed online at
www.freespiritfabrics.com

KAFFE FASSETT

for

FreeSpirit

FreeSpirit Fabrics
Carmel Park II
11121 Carmel Commons Blvd, Ste 280
Charlotte, NC 28226
Tel: (001) 866 907 3305
Email: info@freespiritfabrics.com

The Taunton Press

An imprint of ABRAMS
abramsbooks.com

OTHER DISTRIBUTORS AND STOCKISTS

For Aurifil threads:
Aurifil Italy SRL
www.aurifil.com

Picture framer (see page 40)
Thou Art in Hampstead
106 Mill Lane
London
NW6 1NF
www.thouartframing.co.uk

BACKING AND BINDING FABRICS FOR QUILT TOPS

Cool Bordered Diamonds
Backing: Millefiore Blue QBGP006
Binding: Mad Plaid Plum PWBM037

Mossy Bordered Diamonds
Backing: Japanese Chrysanthemum Magenta QBPJ003
Binding: Zigzag Aqua PWBM043

Contrast Diamonds
Backing: Van Gogh Black QBPJ006
Binding: Jumble Turquoise PWBM053

Hot Diamonds
Backing: Bekah Magenta QBGP012
Binding: Mad Plaid Maroon PWBM037

Warm Roman Tiles
Backing: Bekah Magenta QBGP012
Binding: ZigZag Warm PWBM043

Dark Roman Tiles
Backing: Van Gogh Black QBPJ006
Binding: Reflections Putty PWBM087

Rosy Medallion
Backing: Paperweight Purple QBGP011
Binding: Jumble Magenta PWBM053

Soft Pastel Medallion
Backing: Millefiore Pastel QBGP006
Binding: Jumble Rose PWBM053

Contrast Snowball Stars
Backing: Onion Rings Black QBBM001
Binding: Reflections Sky PWBM087

Hot Snowball Circles
Backing: Japanese Chrysanthemum Magenta QBPJ003
Binding: Flower Dot Warm PWBM077

Hot Economy
Backing: Bekah Magenta QBGP012
Binding: Mad Plaid Maroon PWBM037

Cool Economy
Backing: Millefiore Blue QBGP006
Binding: Jumble Ocean PWBM053

Russet Chevron Stripes
Backing and binding: Pick any Exotic Stripe for both

Leafy Triangles and Stripes
Backing and binding: Pick any Woven Stripe for both

ACKNOWLEDGMENTS

For the photography location for this book, I would like to thank my neighbourhood community at Camden Lock Market and its wonderful mural painters, as well as the houseboat owners on the Regent's Canal.

My greatest gratitude goes, as ever, to our brilliant quilt-making teams: Janet Haigh, with stitchers Ilaria Padovani and Julie Harvey in the UK and Liza Lucy, with stitchers Mira Mayer, Bobbi Penniman, Emilija Mayer Gross and Betsey Westover in the USA. We are also grateful to Judy Irish and Mary-Jane Hutchinson for their excellent quilting.

Grateful thanks go as always to Bundle Backhouse for her diligent technical editing, to Anne Wilson for her beautiful layouts and to the immensely talented eye of our photographer Debbie Patterson. Many thanks, too, to Susan Berry, for managing the process through to print, along with Jen Dorsey and the team at our new publishers, Abrams Books.

Special thanks to Brandon Mably for overseeing everything at the studio from first inspiration to quilt location photography and to the wonderful Dorothy Hill, who so ably and cheerfully assists us in the studio.

QUILT DESIGNERS, MAKERS AND QUILTERS

USA team

Dark Diamonds Kaffe Fassett: designer; Bobbi Penniman: maker; Judy Irish: quilter
Contrast Diamonds Kaffe Fassett: designer; Betsey Westover: maker
Hot Diamonds Kaffe Fassett: designer; Liza Prior Lucy: maker
Soft Pastel Medallion Liza Prior Lucy: designer and maker
Moody Snowball Criss Cross Liza Prior Lucy: designer; Mira Mayer: maker; Judy Irish: quilter
Hot Snowball Circles Liza Prior Lucy: designer; Emilija Mayer Gross: maker
Contrast Snowball Stars Liza Prior Lucy: designer and maker
Cool Economy Kaffe Fassett: designer; Liza Prior Lucy: maker
Contrast Chevron Stripes Kaffe Fassett: designer; Liza Prior Lucy: maker; Judy Irish: quilter
Russet Chevron Stripes Kaffe Fassett: designer; Liza Prior Lucy: maker
Leafy Triangles and Stripes Kaffe Fassett: designer; Liza Prior Lucy: maker

UK team

Bright Bordered Diamonds Kaffe Fassett: designer; Julie Harvey: maker; Mary-Jane Hutchinson: quilter
Cool Bordered Diamonds Kaffe Fassett: designer; Julie Harvey: maker
Mossy Bordered Diamonds Kaffe Fassett: designer; Julie Harvey: maker
Contrast Roman Tiles Kaffe Fassett: designer; Ilaria Padovani: maker; Mary-Jane Hutchinson: quilter
Warm Roman Tiles Kaffe Fassett: designer; Ilaria Padovani: maker
Dark Roman Tiles Kaffe Fassett: designer; Ilaria Padovani: maker
Rich Dark Medallion Kaffe Fassett: designer; Julie Harvey: maker; Mary-Jane Hutchinson: quilter
Rosy Medallion Kaffe Fassett: designer; Ilaria Padovani: maker
Green Economy Kaffe Fassett: designer; Julie Harvey: maker; Mary-Jane Hutchinson: quilter
Hot Economy Kaffe Fassett: designer; Ilaria Padovani: maker
Triangles and Stripes Cushions Kaffe Fassett: designer; Dorothy Hill: maker